endorsements

"This *Guide* is for all theological educators, religion scholars, and graduate students who wish to publish intentionally and strategically for their professional advancement and vocational goals. The authors offer practical advice and make nuanced and important distinctions for publishing in religious and theological studies. The stakes are high, and knowing where you are, or where you want to go, should guide your publishing decisions. This book will help you make choices based on your goals and context in and along the institutional spectrum of theological education and the academic study of religion. If you are a graduate student or early-career scholar, the authors provide up-to-date advice you may not get from mentors or advisors. If you have been at this for a while and have already published—a senior or mid-career scholar—times have changed, and this enchiridion will help you, too."

— JOHN F. KUTSKO, EXECUTIVE DIRECTOR, SOCIETY OF BIBLICAL LITERATURE

"It has taken me two decades to learn by personal experience—trial and error, manuscript by manuscript, publisher by publisher—all of the wisdom contained in this guide, and I am not sure why something like this has not been put together before. Now it's available, and faculty facing a daunting and dynamic field of theological and religious studies publishing can be heartened that they have a companion to chart first steps along the way."

—AMOS YONG, PROFESSOR OF THEOLOGY AND MISSION, AND DEAN, SCHOOL OF THEOLOGY AND SCHOOL OF INTERCULTURAL STUDIES, FULLER SEMINARY

"Too often, junior and senior scholars alike find the publishing process daunting and confusing. Kostova and Alexander demystify that process, illuminating the differences between publishers, exploring the financial and contractual models employed by publishing firms, and laying out a roadmap to move the reader from an initial project concept through a well-constructed proposal to a successful publication.

—ROBERT A. RATCLIFF, EXECUTIVE EDITOR, WESTMINSTER JOHN KNOX PRESS

"A helpful and current addition to the resources available to scholars of religion, particularly those with theological interests. All fields need this kind of resource."

— ALICE HUNT, EXECUTIVE DIRECTOR, AMERICAN ACADEMY OF RELIGION

"This is the most comprehensive, contextualized, and concise publishing guide I have come across in my twenty plus years of supporting Latinx scholars in religion and theology. It provides scholars with a helpful list of publishing venues and a clear way forward to begin their publishing careers. Can't wait to share it with HTI scholars."

— REVEREND JOANNE RODRÍGUEZ, EXECUTIVE DIRECTOR,
HISPANIC THEOLOGICAL INITIATIVE

BUILDING A
scholarly
CAREER

The ATS Guide to
Religious and Theological Publishing

JULIA K. KOSTOVA
PATRICK H. ALEXANDER

Published in the United States of America in 2019 by
The Association of Theological Schools
10 Summit Park Dr., Pittsburgh, PA 15275
www.ats.edu

ISBN 978-0-578-55678-9

Printed in the United States of America.

BUILDING A

scholarly

CAREER

The ATS Guide to
Religious and Theological Publishing

TABLE OF CONTENTS

you're going to need a map

In the academic career, teaching, service, and publishing are often the three yardsticks by which scholars are measured for promotion, tenure, or professional advancement. In many instances, publishing may be third on the list; in others, it is all that matters. Ordinarily, research institutions place a premium on publishing, but not just any publishing: you must publish in the accepted venues. Religiously affiliated seminaries, colleges, and universities range in their expectations; institutions with historic ties to denominations likewise may vary. Not all institutions, schools, colleges, or seminaries will require publishing for tenure and promotion to the same degree, but it is critical to know the lay of the land. And, if you want to be published, you need to know how important choosing the right publisher(s) for your work can be. Thus, Evangel University, for example, an Assemblies of God liberal arts university, states in its faculty handbook that to obtain tenure, faculty must give evidence of efforts to maintain and strengthen professional skills through active participation in local, state, and national professional organizations and through other scholarly endeavors.[1]

This is one criterion for tenure in a list of eight. While "scholarly endeavors" alludes to publishing, it is less clear as to what value publishing holds in this context, especially as compared to the other seven criteria.

Compare the statement above with Duke University's 2017 *Faculty Handbook*:

> Tenure at Duke University, whether awarded to a faculty member currently on the Duke faculty or offered to a scholar who is being recruited for the Duke faculty, should be reserved for those who have clearly demonstrated through their performance as scholars and teachers that their work has been widely perceived among their peers as outstanding. Persons holding the rank of associate professor with tenure are expected to stand in competition with the foremost persons of similar rank in similar fields and to show clear evidence of continuing excellence in scholarly activity in their years at the university. Good teaching and university service should be expected but cannot in and of themselves be sufficient grounds for tenure.[2]

It must be noted that these requirements include the divinity school, and this holds true at most university-related divinity schools or schools of theology. The last sentence is telling: "Good teaching and university service should be expected but cannot in and of themselves be sufficient grounds for tenure."

Fewer students are enrolling in theological degree programs, although paradoxically, the twenty-first century has witnessed the opening of new schools. In the competitive academic environment, institutions of all stripes increasingly put value on publishing outcomes of faculty, and scholars with a robust publishing record would be better positioned to succeed. This holds especially true in "mainline" groups that have

---

1   Faculty and Administration Handbook, Evangel University (2013), 35. https://www.evangel.edu/wp-content/uploads/2017/01/FacultyHandbook.pdf. Accessed on July 21, 2019.
2   *Duke University Faculty Handbook* (2017), ch. 3, 2. https://provost.duke.edu/sites/all/files/FHB.pdf. Accessed on July 21, 2019.

❝ Despite the prominent role of publishing in the academic career, graduate students and faculty do not always receive training and information about how to get published.

rigorous qualifications for ministers, priests, rabbis, and pastors. Further, moving across denominational and institutional lines will require a strong publishing track record that accords with those institutions' performance expectations.

So, questions such as "Where am I?" and "Where do I want to be in my career five years from now?" figure vitally into a publishing strategy. For many, serving in a denominational context is their clear calling. Others may not be quite sure where they will be in five years. Regardless, it will be essential to align your work with your institution's expectations. The demand to publish will only increase, so you will want to know what kind of material counts for tenure and promotion and which publishing venues are valued. Early career scholars with a different future in mind must know what kind of publishing matters in their immediate context, and if they imagine a career path that takes them to other destinations (e.g., liberal arts colleges or a seminary), they should investigate the publishing expectations at those institutions and plan accordingly. At the heart, this involves learning which publishers matter for one's career path, because choosing the wrong publisher can limit your career choices down the road.

Despite the prominent role of publishing in the academic career, graduate students and faculty do not always receive training and information about how to get published. Furthermore, given the swiftly evolving publishing landscape, the options and challenges that early-career researchers today will face differ greatly from those of their senior colleagues.

Given the imbrication between the scholarly career and publishing, we would like to start with a brief overview of the state of the scholarly publishing industry in religious studies and demonstrate how the changes that are reshaping the industry are affecting scholars' publishing choices—

3

and, consequently, their professional success.

Many of our readers will have heard of and even experienced firsthand the disruptive technological, economic, policy, and structural changes that scholarly publishing is undergoing. The shrinking library budget, for example, is a familiar topic to both faculty and publishers. According to a revealing report by the Association of Research Libraries (ARL), between 1984 and 2011, the percentage of funding universities spent on libraries declined steeply from 3.4 to 1.7 percent of total expenditure.[3] In fact, and partially in response to changing research habits that have moved online, libraries are shifting away from building collections in favor of providing access to electronic resources. A report published in 2017, for example, estimates that only 22 percent of academic library budgets has been spent on print books[4]; some libraries have even redesigned their spaces, trans- forming them from spaces where researchers could browse through the stacks into a series of points-of-access stations.

Academic libraries used to be the main and most reliable buyer of schol- arly publications like monographs. Shrinking library budgets are one of the major factors that have forced publishers to rethink their editorial strategy—i.e., what manuscripts they acquire—as they can no longer rely on increasingly underfunded research libraries.

Further, many of you have read about bookstores closing all over the US. Large chains like Borders and independent bookshops alike have been forced to close by stiff competition from online retailers, which can afford to lower prices below those of brick-and-mortar booksellers. Es- timates of the number of bookstore closings over the past decade vary widely, but, notwithstanding the recent resurgence of indie bookstores in urban areas,[5] the bookshelf space has shrunk dramatically, meaning that it has become harder for publishers to sell books, which in turn is forcing

---

3   ARL Statistics Survey, Association of Research Libraries (ARL), (2013), http://www.libqual.org/documents/admin/ EG_2.pdf. The ARL statistics and surveys can be found here https://www.arl.org/arl-statistics-salary-survey/ and here http://www.arlstatistics.org/about/Series/stats_series. Accessed July 21, 2019.

4   Matt Enis, "LJ Study: Electronic Resources Continue Steady Gains in Academic Libraries," *Library Journal*, last modi- fied March 3, 2018. https://www.libraryjournal.com/?detailStory=lj-study-electronic-resources-continue-steady-gains.

5   Andrea Cheng, "Bookstores Find Growth as 'Anchors of Authenticity'," *New York Times*, modified June 23, 2019. https://www.nytimes.com/2019/06/23/business/independent-bookstores.html

them to modulate their acquisition strategies. New players in the book publishing and selling space, like Amazon—now the largest bookseller in the world, distributing at least two-thirds of all books worldwide—have further disrupted the scholarly publishing model and added new pressures on scholarly publishers.

❝ This publishing guide is designed to help you navigate the changing landscape and to equip you with the knowledge to craft a successful publishing strategy that fits your professional circumstances and that meets your publishing objectives.

What all of this has meant is that highly specialized monographs are not judged solely by their scholarly value; their economic potential plays a more important role than in previous times. For scholars to build a successful publishing record, it is important to understand what publishers look for when they evaluate manuscripts.

The changes in the scholarly publishing market are accompanied by changes in the academic environment. The scholarly landscape is becoming a lot more competitive, partially due to the supply of PhDs outstripping the growth of jobs. One of the effects of that is that scholars, even those at the beginning of their careers, are increasingly expected to have a robust publications record. Similarly, at many institutions the bar for tenure is rising, and so is the pressure to publish more, early, and frequently.

In short, the conditions in which scholars are expected to thrive grow tougher and more competitive; a publishing track record plays an ever-increasing role for tenure, promotion, and professional advancement at a time when the industry is being reshaped by external and internal forces. This *Guide*, written specially with scholars in theological and religious studies in mind whose academic career advancement depends on publications, is designed to help you navigate the changing landscape and to equip you with the knowledge to craft a successful publishing strategy that fits your professional circumstances and that meets your publishing objectives.

How to use this guide

The *Guide* assumes that you—a scholar of religious and theological studies—understand that publishing will be a central component of a successful career. It assumes that you need a publishing strategy. It further assumes that the publishing ecosystem of religious and theological publishing is unique because the publishing landscape is complicated by the fact that theological and religious perspectives differ and the publishers in this broad discipline reflect this complexity. Thus, the *Guide* is a resource tailored for The Association of Theological Schools to help its constituency accomplish several objectives: (1) The *Guide* and the accompanying taxonomy of publishers in the space of religious and theological studies can assist you in identifying the best publisher for your work, that is, those publishers whose subject areas match yours as a researcher and those publishers that count for your career objectives as a scholar (i.e., meet the expectations of tenure and promotion). (2) The *Guide* will also give you insight into how to approach the publisher(s) that you have identified as appropriate for your project. (3) The *Guide* and the accompanying taxonomy of publishers in the space of religious and theological studies will provide valuable information for constructing your career strategy both in your existing context and in the context of where you want to be in your career in five years.

CHAPTER TWO

you've got to have a plan

The importance of having a publishing strategy

Arguably anyone in academia, whether the hard sciences or the broad liberal arts, needs a publications strategy. Even at institutions that value teaching, publishing remains the anchor to which one ties the climbing rope. And should you decide to move upwardly or laterally, that anchor will be in play. The idea that you might wish to move during your career should come as no surprise. First, opportunities to teach within denominational and interdenominational contexts are diminishing, especially in North America.[6] Second, people who study religion and theology may change

---

6   ATS *Annual Report* (2016). https://www.ats.edu/uploads/resources/publications-presentations/documents/2016-annual-report.pdf. Accessed on July 21, 2019.

> **"** Having a publishing strategy should be a factor in assessing your career and where you want to be in five or ten or twenty years.

their perspectives as time goes by. Changing attitudes toward doctrinal positions, an unexpected shift in family circumstances, the pressure of financial needs, or other life events may lead us to new opportunities. Third, as intimated above, theological schools with higher profiles (e.g., Yale, Duke, Perkins, Candler, Vanderbilt) have *greater* expectations for publishing performance. Moving across denominational or institutional lines will require a stronger publishing track record that accords with those institutions' expectations. Consequently, in the face of these realities, it falls to the scholar to "expect the unexpected" when it comes to your career. Having a publishing strategy should be a factor in assessing your career and where you want to be in five or ten or twenty years. Your choices today will either open or close doors in your future. Good choices about publishing will not ensure success, but poor choices will almost certainly frustrate it.

In the fields of religious and theological publishing, answering (or not) beforehand the questions of what you publish and where you publish can dramatically affect your career. Your publishing choices should align with your career goals, because publishing in the *wrong* place may have unintended consequences down the road. Moreover, knowing when to publish—that is, being aware of your tenure "clock" and how that clock relates to the actual time it takes to get published (think years, not months)—must always be kept in mind. Poor time management—waiting too late to start on a project—has led to the end of more than a few careers. The importance of formulating a publishing strategy should become clearer as you explore the types of publishing and how these fit into a plan. Essential to that strategy is knowing how to publish, what to publish, and where to publish.

Developing a publishing strategy for your career

We've emphasized the importance of having a publishing strategy that fits with your career circumstances and aspirations. The changing landscape of the scholarly publishing industry, as well as the increased competition in academia and emphasis on publishing outcomes, necessitates having a robust, long-term publishing strategy. When building your strategic publishing plan, consider the following:

1) Know what counts.

Knowing *concretely* what is expected of you and what your objectives are for your next tenure and promotion event is critical for developing your publishing strategy. Requirements—as well as who determines those—vary by institution and/or department, and so do your own circumstances. Some institutions require a published monograph; others would accept a book contract, essays in edited collections, or articles in peer-reviewed journals. It is critical for you to understand what the requirements are at your institution and, consequently, what counts, as well as what your objectives should be. It is particularly important to strategically balance all the obligations that academic life places in front of faculty (teaching, committee work, reviewing, writing, etc.) at the beginning of your career. As you work toward tenure, make sure to focus on the projects that align with your goals in the context of your institutional requirements. Remember that you are not alone in this process. Your academic dean, the chair of your department, mentors, and other people at your institution and community can offer guidance and advice, and resources like this *Guide* and the accompanying taxonomy included at the back of this book can further support you in your journey.

Whatever the specific publication deliverables, chances are that many of you will be required to publish peer-reviewed publications, and therefore we'd like to take a moment to discuss peer review.

66 Your academic dean, the chair of your department, mentors, and other people at your institution and community can offer guidance and advice, and resources like this *Guide* can further support you in your journey.

Peer review is the cornerstone of scholarship and scholarly publishing, validating the originality, intellectual soundness, and contribution of new research. It is a part of your academic career and key to your publishing strategy. It is worth noting, however, that there is no universal standard of peer review; it will vary by discipline and field. The most common types of peer review include single-blind (i.e., the reviewer knows the author's identity but the reviewer's anonymity is preserved), double-blind[7] (neither the author nor the reviewer knows the other's identity), open peer review (the reviewer's identity is publicly disclosed), and post-publication peer review (comments after publication supplant pre-publication peer review). Double-blind peer review for journals and single-blind for books/monographs are most commonly used in the humanities, but, again, peer review varies within the different subdisciplines and even by project. As scholars working in the space of religious and theological studies, you must know the gold standard in your field and ensure that the projects you're committed to meet the peer-review standards of your institution.[8]

2) Have a timetable.

Knowing in advance what you are expected to deliver for your next tenure and promotion review will also help you create a timetable. Publishing a book or a journal article is a long-term project. Research and writing can take months and even years; post-submission work, like peer review (which, for book manuscripts, can take up to four months or more)

---

7   To avoid the use of the term *blind* in describing the peer review process, which disability experts have cautioned can be offensive, ATS has instead adopted the use of *anonymous*.

8   The Association of University Presses' *Best Practices for Peer Review Guide* can be downloaded here: https://is.gd/Bg2dd0.

and revisions, adds several months more; and the actual production for a book can vary anywhere between six months and a year. Submissions in prestigious journals that receive a high number of submissions can also take months. Adding those up means that the publication lifecycle of a book or an article in a well-reputed journal can take up to two to three years. This information is important to know when you consider your tenure clock. How much time do you have until your next tenure and promotion review? What are the expectations? Are there any intermediate steps that you need to take into account and to start working toward?

3) Know your publishing options.

Given the many types of publishers and publishing opportunities that you are likely to encounter in the course of your career, in the sections below, we look at the types of publishing projects most typically available to scholars specifically in religious and theological studies, and discuss how to strategically assess their value in light of your personal career goals. We also present a taxonomy of the types of publishers in religious and theological studies designed to help you understand how each fits with your career and to guide you in identifying potential publishers for your work. (See also the taxonomy map on the inside back cover.)

CHAPTER THREE

types of publishing opportunities

The typical academic career encompasses a wide range of publication types. Many of you will have written reference or encyclopedia articles, will have edited or contributed to edited collections, will be striving toward publishing a monograph at the beginning of your careers, and will possibly aim for impact or trade books at some point in your careers. In this section, we look at the types of publishing opportunities, the most common of which are listed below, and offer suggestions to evaluate and balance those choices in the context of your career goals and strategic publishing objectives.

Dissertations

For many PhD programs in the humanities, a dissertation is a requirement for completing the PhD. The dissertation's chief aim is to demonstrate the candidate's skills in doing intellectually robust research, as is visible in the detailed documentation of research in a typically extensive scholarly apparatus. The dissertation is the mark of a completed apprenticeship. From that point of view, the best dissertation is the completed dissertation.

Monographs

A monograph is a detailed, long-form study of a specialized topic. A monograph is often required for tenure in the humanities. It used to be that the dissertation would get revised and published as a first monograph. But with industry and market changes forcing publishers to look for books with a broader appeal, this option has become less frequently available.

Scholarly books and academic trade

"Scholarly," "impact," or "academic trade" refer to book profiles; publishers use those profiles to characterize and describe book projects and, based on them, develop projections and editorial, sales, or marketing plans. Unlike monographs, which are highly specialized and therefore accessible to a limited audience of experts, the profiles listed here refer to book projects with a wider readership potential. In scholarly and academic trade publications, the author's ability to use his or her existing platform also is a crucial consideration. Authors should embrace the roles they can play in expanding the audience for their work, chiefly by broadening the topic and writing in accessible and engaging prose that would appeal to a wider audience, such as scholars from other fields or disciplines.

Journal articles

Peer-reviewed articles in scholarly journals offer a venue to publish shorter but still well-developed ideas on a specialized topic. Journal articles can be a first foray into a new research topic—and a great way to test a new theory—that can later serve as a basis for a larger work or body of research. In general, articles in peer-reviewed journals that present

66 Authors should embrace the roles they can play in expanding the audience for their work, chiefly by broadening the topic and writing in accessible and engaging prose that would appeal to a wider audience.

new research and analysis (as different from review articles, for example, or other synthetic article types sometimes published in journals) count toward your publication record. Further, in some disciplines and even subdisciplines, especially in the social sciences and the sciences, the journal article is the main unit of currency.

Edited collections

It is likely that at some point in your career you will be asked to participate in an edited collection, either as a contributor or as an editor. While edited collections don't always count toward your publication record, they nonetheless offer valuable opportunities to work with your colleagues and to be a part of your research community. With regard to editing a collection, given the amount of work and effort involved, you should think carefully about taking on such a project, especially if still untenured. In other words, it is important to balance the "political" and networking benefits with the value assigned to edited collections in the promotion and tenure process in your current or future contexts.

From a publishing point of view, edited collections are becoming harder to sustain economically, and therefore hard to sell to a publisher, so again be careful not to spend too much of your time on those at the expense of the activities that count toward your publication record.

❝ Think strategically about the opportunities you select and consider how your choices align with your publishing strategy and career objectives.

Textbooks, classroom supplements, and other pedagogical materials

Teaching materials are incredibly valuable pedagogic tools and are terrific ways to support your teaching, but because they distill—rather than advance—knowledge, they normally would not count toward your publication record. With this in mind, be careful to balance the time and energy you devote to developing and pitching such materials versus other publications that would help you achieve your goal.

Reference works

Some fields (e.g., musicology) have very well-reputed, field-defining reference works. Religious studies also has a long history of reference works of lasting impact (e.g., Eliade's *Encyclopedia of Religion*). Notwithstanding that, reference contributions would typically not count toward tenure and promotion, because they are synthetic in nature and do not advance knowledge. That said, as with edited collections, there are often good reasons to participate (e.g., to be a part of your community), to contribute to innovative projects, or to expand the readership on your topic.

Magazine and denominational articles

Many in theological and religious studies are interested in building a readership beyond academic audiences. Writing in magazines and other publications with broader readership can therefore be an attractive opportunity, even though they are likely not to be counted toward tenure.

Book reviews

Book reviews are a good way to cut your teeth as a writer and a critic and to build up your CV. Yet, because they typically don't undergo the rigorous peer review that is the hallmark of scholarly value, they carry little weight for tenure and promotion.

Blogs, vlogs, and digital humanities projects

With new media increasingly becoming mainstream in storytelling and analysis, the number of blogs, vlogs, and digital humanities projects has grown, and some have become important forums for exchange of ideas outside of the traditional venues of academic discourse. Universities are still grappling with how to assess those, and policies vary.

The list above of publishing opportunities that you will encounter in the course of your career is by no means exhaustive or fixed; our aim here isn't so much to offer a comprehensive catalog as to encourage you to think strategically about the opportunities you select and to consider how your choices align with your publishing strategy and career objectives.

CHAPTER FOUR

the landscape

of scholarly religious and theological publishing and your scholarly career

This section offers and interprets a taxonomy of academic religious and theological publishers, chiefly within the Judeo-Christian traditions and mainly among English-language publishers. (Some attention to Spanish will be given as well as to German, Dutch, and Belgian publishers.) Book publishers figure prominently, but many, especially societies or associations, commercial and institutional publishers, and university presses, also publish peer-reviewed journals. Publishing in journals can be essential for a career and should not be overlooked. Numerous types of religious and theological publishers and information providers exist, serving different audiences and missions, but not all are important for an academic career. One need only contrast the American Academy of Religion/Society of Biblical Literature (AAR/SBL) exhibit with that of the Christian Booksellers Association (CBA): Publishing represented by CBA mainly seeks publications for a general audience that address practical issues,

> **"** By matching your work with the publisher that counts for your career ahead of time, you will save time and energy in your search to find the right publisher.

self-help books, Bible study, and worship resources, whereas the AAR/ SBL's publications are exclusively in the scholarly realm. For the purposes of this *Guide*, which focuses on building a scholarly career, we will look at scholarly publishers occupying the religious and theological studies space. Thus, when we speak of denominational publishers, we mean especially those that have a commitment to higher education and that expect faculty to publish. Plus, we're doing this in the context of how publishing factors into a scholarly career.

As we noted earlier, in chapter 1, both small and large institutions expect their faculty to publish in order to secure tenure and advance in their careers. Moreover, institutions expect faculty to publish the *right* kind of work in the *right* place (see the section below on identifying the right publisher). Scholars working in the broad and wide-ranging area of religious studies—from biblical archaeology to scripture exegesis to art history—face unique career decisions when it comes to publishing. This is especially the case with anyone working in the context of seminaries, rabbinical colleges, divinity schools, and graduate schools of religion. While senior scholars often experience a greater freedom to write for a broader public, for early career scholars who may be in the process of determining a career path, a lot can ride on making the correct choice when it comes to a publisher.

The taxonomy below is designed to assist researchers in evaluating and placing their work in a way that will maximize its value for tenure and promotion. By matching your work with the publisher that counts for your career ahead of time, you will save time and energy in your search to find the right publisher. The taxonomy covers publishers that play a role in an academic setting (i.e., for tenure and promotion), specifically denominational, interdenominational, non-denominational, trade religion, commercial religion, institutional/society publishers, and university presses. We also discuss several other miscellaneous types of publishers that scholars can encounter and touch on the recent phenomenon of self-publishing. A map, included on the inside back cover of this *Guide*, follows this structure.

66 By using this *Guide*, you should be able to place your work within the context of the categories above and in the context of your career path.

Broadly speaking, the presses in the categories above share common features. Not all will fit neatly into a single category, and many presses will have a clear presence in another category. Thus, a university press might also have "trade religion" titles. Further, it is important to remember that, as the field evolves, publishers' interests can also change over time, as presses are bought and sold, as denominations evolve and refocus their visions, and as religions embrace or wrestle with new social and cultural topics such as artificial intelligence, science, politics, education, and so on. The categories offered in this *Guide* should not be viewed as fixed, and publishers can take on the qualities of more than one of these categories. Further, the list is not exhaustive but, rather, representative of the publishers operating in the space of religious and theological studies that typically matter in an academic setting. Thus, it does not cover in detail "vocational" presses, which have a different audience and emphasis.

By using this *Guide*, you should be able to place your work within the context of the categories above and in the context of your career path. We follow below this basic structure: description, examples, and how the category relates to your career. This will save valuable time, maximize the

21

chances of success, and assist in building a strategy consistent with institutional requirements and the scholar's career schedule. Before delving into the taxonomy itself, it might be helpful to remember, as we underscored earlier, that scholars should always keep in mind the relevance of this taxonomy for charting a career path, for securing tenure and promotion, given your institution's expectations, and for finding an advantage in this highly competitive knowledge marketplace.

Denominational publishers

The chart included on the inside back cover of the *Guide* mainly includes US denominational publishing houses. Denominational publishers for our purposes are those publishers whose primary mission is to train ministers and other religious workers and to meet the needs of a denomination by publishing books, classroom materials, periodicals, and other literature to advance the educational, theological, and missional goals of the denomination. Denominational houses that focus on one denomination often have a credentialing role in higher education. The purpose of this credentialing may include valuing doctrinal and theological allegiance over controversial or critical scholarship.

Topics published typically include pastoral care and counseling, church and denominational histories, Bible studies, prayer, doctrinal studies, leadership, and youth and children's ministry. Most of the publications are distributed directly to congregations and churches. Publications may or may not be found on Amazon.com. A few denominational publishing houses have been known to publish for audiences outside their denominations. For example, the Gospel Publishing House of the Assemblies of God is known worldwide for its acclaimed book *The Joy of Signing*. Herald Press, a trade imprint (i.e., a discrete brand of a publishing house) of the Mennonite church, invites authors outside of the Amish and Mennonite tradition. But, generally speaking, denominational publishing houses publish for denominational purposes. Catholic and Jewish publishers also serve their constituents, but their missions include ecumenical works as well as books focused on Catholic or Jewish theology and practice. The names of denominational presses and non-denominational presses can be confusing, so care should be taken because denominations look for conformity to doctrine. Beacon Hill Press, for instance, was formerly a publisher for the Nazarene Church, while Beacon Press is affiliated with the Unitarian Universalist Association. Review and Herald serves Seventh-Day Adventists, but Herald Press targets Mennonites/Anabaptists. Cascadia Publishing House is Mennonite/Anabaptist, while Cascade Books is an imprint of Wipf & Stock. Brigham Young University Press and Andrews University Press are denominational publishers and are not members of the Association of University Presses.

Let's look at the denominational presses on the map at the back of this *Guide*:

Brigham Young University Press (Jesus Christ of Latter-Day Saints)—Provo, UT. Not a member of the Association of University Presses, BYU Press publishes chiefly works related to the history of the denomination, to the text of the *Book of Mormon*, to the New Testament, and to the theological and doctrinal positions of the Church of Jesus Christ of Latter-Day Saints. Online, *The Encyclopedia of Mormonism* covers topics ranging from Aaron, the brother of Moses, to the Zoramites, mentioned in the *Book of Mormon*.

Cascadia Publishing House (Anabaptist and Mennonite)—Telford, PA. Cascadia promotes itself thus: "Supporting examination of faith, history, and contemporary life from an Anabaptist perspective, Cascadia Publishing House LLC is an Anabaptist-Mennonite publisher serving Anabaptist, Mennonite, Christian, and general readers."[9] Unlike Warner Press and Gospel Publishing House, which focus on publishing for the faithful in those respective denominations, Cascadia intends to reach beyond an Anabaptist–Mennonite perspective. Consider, for example,

---

9 https://www.cascadiapublishinghouse.com/.

Paul Alexander's volume *Peace to War: Shifting Allegiances in the Assemblies of God*, which documents the devolution of the Assemblies of God from an originally pacifist movement to a denomination that fully embraces Americanism and endorses nationalistic and militaristic practices. Cascadia's interest in peace and justice issues invites researchers beyond denominational borders.

COGIC Publishing House (Church of God in Christ)—Memphis, TN. COGIC publishes resources for Christian living, Sunday School curriculum, music ministry, denominational history, and Bible study. These topics stand at the center of the publishing mission of this Holiness-Pentecostal denomination founded in 1897 by Bishop C. H. Mason.

Concordia Publishing House (Lutheran Church–Missouri Synod)—St. Louis, MO. Concordia Publishing House publishes essentially for its constituency, although its multivolume *Luther's Works* would be a primary resource for studying Martin Luther's writings for non-Lutherans as well as Lutherans. But essentially its professional and scholarly publications, such as the Concordia Commentary Series, are designed for Lutheran clergy and laypersons. The Evangelical Lutheran Church, USA's counterpart to Concordia is Augsburg Fortress Press.

Gospel Publishing House (Assemblies of God)—Springfield, MO. GPH publishes mainly denominational materials in English and Spanish. GPH publications focus on teaching resources for different types of ministry (children, youth, adult), preaching, and Christian living, and they emphasize Assemblies of God doctrine and practice. AG Publishers, an imprint of GPH, publishes denominational histories (Azusa Street Series) that tell the story of the denomination's origins.

Herald Press (Mennonite Church)—Harrisonburg, VA. According to its website, "Herald Press is the trade book imprint of MennoMedia, an agency of Mennonite Church USA and Mennonite Church Canada." Although Herald Press remains committed to its denominational roots (e.g., peacemaking), its publications also aim for a wider audience, as exemplified in its *Believers' Church Bible Commentary*, in which scholars write for both lay and pastoral audiences.

Review and Herald Publishing Association (Seventh-Day Adventist)—Hagerstown, MD. Now under the umbrella of Pacific Press, Review and Herald focuses on resources for Adventists and other Christians. Familiar topics such as prayer, music, Bible study, children and youth ministry, and Christian living complement the centerpiece of Review and Herald/Pacific Press, the writings of Ellen G. White, such as *Conflict of the Ages* and *Christ's Object Lessons*.

Warner Press (Church of God)—Anderson, IN. Similarly to Gospel Publishing House, Warner Press publishes mainly church curriculum materials, books on Christian living, and Bible studies that are designed to promote discipleship and faithful living and to encourage those going through difficult times. Resources are tailored for ministers and practitioners across various age groups, and many are available in either English or Spanish.

Denominational publishing houses and your career

Without question, denominational institutions—whether liberal arts colleges or graduate schools of religion or seminaries—expect their faculty to publish. Statements as to what exactly is required are not always easy to find, and where they are found, they may lack specificity. For faculty publishing at a seminary, for instance, requirements will vary according to the denomination. Denominations may expect their faculty to publish with the denominational publishing house; others may not. For some, publishing within a denominational context will make sense, but for others, a decision to publish with a denominational press could short-circuit other career objectives if the denominational press focuses only on denominational issues. The researcher must know exactly what is expected in a denominational context. One size does not fit all. Moreover, denominational faculty who may be teaching at interdenominational schools like

Gordon-Conwell Theological Seminary or Fuller Theological Seminary or at denominational institutions must choose wisely, balancing denominational requirements with institutional expectations.

Interdenominational publishers [10]

This category includes denominationally based houses whose publishing "list" may include denominationally focused publications but whose publishing programs extend beyond the denomination. A "list" is the topical focus or the subject areas a press covers. Some presses specialize in one area; others have expansive lists. Let's review the interdenominational presses on the map located on the inside back cover of this *Guide*:

❝ If you plan to work in a religiously affiliated liberal arts college, seminary, or graduate school of religion, choosing an interdenominational publishing house could be a wise choice.

Abingdon Press (United Methodist Church)—Nashville, TN. Abingdon Press, an imprint of the United Methodist Publishing House, following a merger between the Methodist Episcopal Church South and the Evangelical United Brethren Methodist Church in 1968, began publishing "a wide array of high-caliber academic, professional, inspirational, and life-affirming religious literature to enrich church communities across the globe" (see its website). Abingdon, thus, does publish books about

---

10   The authors use "interdenominational" in the title of this section at the recommendation of The Association of Theological Schools (ATS). Many ATS schools and faculty are engaged in, and have long-held commitments to, interreligious dialogue. While a different title would help to decenter protestant Christian privilege, we have kept "denominational" in three of the categories to highlight the reality that the boundaries one must consider in building a career publishing strategy typically run along confessional lines (e.g., Reformed or Holiness, Pentecostal or Baptist) rather than religious lines (e.g., Jewish or Christian or Hindi or Sikh, Catholic or Orthodox).

Christian living, prayer, Methodist teachings, Bible study, and inspirational resources, but it also has an academic line whose authors come from a wide variety of denominational and confessional contexts. Abingdon's biblical commentary series includes authors from Earlham School of Religion, the Weston Jesuit School of Theology, and Southern Methodist University, as well as Boston College (also a Jesuit school). Many of its authors teach at public or private universities and colleges. The scholarly books published by Abingdon undergo a peer review appropriate to the subject and audience and are not—as denominational houses sometimes can be—evaluated only on the basis of doctrinal or theological conformity.

Andrews University Press (Seventh-Day Adventist)—Berrien Springs, MI. While Andrews University Press publishes volumes for the denomination (theological study, seminary dissertations, the Andrews Study Bible, Adventist Series), it is also known for Hebrew Bible lexical resources, such as Alger F. Johns's *A Short Grammar of Biblical Aramaic* or Oliver Glanz's *Biblical Hebrew Reviewer*. Particularly, Andrews University Press is recognized for its biblical archaeology publications such as numerous volumes on Tell-Hesban, the Madaba Plains Project, Neo-Sumerian Account Texts, and Old Babylonian Account Texts. These latter volumes form part of the scholarly record of the excavation of the Near East.

Augsburg Fortress (Evangelical Lutheran Church of America)—Minneapolis, MN. Augsburg Fortress is the official publisher of the Evangelical Lutheran Church of America. The two presses—Augsburg and Fortress—merged in 1988. Augsburg is known especially for its church-centered publications, while Fortress, which also publishes for the pew, stands out as a scholarly publisher. In its heyday, Fortress was renowned for its list in biblical studies, theology, and church history. Its authors came from a wide variety of faith backgrounds, and in addition to producing highly technical commentaries like *Hermeneia*, Fortress translated scholarly volumes from other languages and figured prominently, along with Westminster John Knox (WJK), in the construction of the religious-theological landscape in North America. Over time, however, the production of scholarly works decreased—for the same reasons that affected all denominations.

Beacon Press (under the auspices of the Unitarian Universalist Association)—Boston, MA. Founded in the mid-nineteenth century, Beacon Press has a sweeping list including history, the environment, African-American studies, queer studies, literature, politics, race, science and medicine, and more. Its impressive religion list emphasizes the major religions of Buddhism, Hinduism, Christianity, Judaism, and Islam, and underscores the role of pluralism and diversity. Beacon Press is an excellent example of a press that fits into different categories. On the scholarly side, Beacon (an associate member of the Association of University Presses) publishes James H. Cone's *Risks of Faith*; but it is perhaps better known as a trade publisher for books like Viktor E. Frankel's *Man's Search for Meaning* or Cornel West's *Race Matters*.

Chalice Press (Disciples of Christ)—Atlanta, GA. Chalice Press authors have a broad theological perspective and seek to serve the layperson, the professional, and the scholar. Many of its volumes address social injustice and the meaning and implications of ministerial practices such as practical theology, preaching, and pastoral care.

Editorial Verbo Divino (Catholic)—various locations. Although many scholarly presses are now publishing in Spanish, and Spain and Latin America have always had scholarly publications, Editorial Verbo Divino, with offices in Argentina, Bolivia, Chile, Colombia, Costa Rica, Mexico, Spain, and the United States, among others, has made a statement of its goals and mission by exhibiting at affairs like the annual American Academy of Religion/Society of Biblical Literature meeting. The Society of the Divine Word is a religious missionary organization of the Latin Church within the Roman Catholic Church. Its publications range in topic from religion and society to biblical studies, church history, and pastoral resources. It has translated into Spanish English-language classics such as Raymond Brown, Joseph Fitzmeyer, and Roland Murphy, eds., *New Jerome Bible Commentary/Nuevo Comentario Bíblico San Jerónimo*.

Hebrew Union College Press (Jewish)—Cincinnati, OH. Publishing both books and journals, HUC Press offers rich resources for language study, Rabbinics, Jewish law, Bible, history, Holocaust studies, and more. It is perhaps best known for the highly respected *Hebrew Union College Annual*. Scholars from around the globe publish with HUC Press. According to its website, publications in all its imprints are peer reviewed.

Jewish Theological Seminary Press (Jewish)—New York, NY. This small press produces scholarly resources for the study and practice of Judaism, including reference works, concordances, grammars, and tractates of the Talmud (in Hebrew) as well as critical editions of Midrashic texts.

KTAV Publishing (Jewish)—New York, NY. KTAV publishes and distributes a wide variety of resources for Jewish studies. Its scholarly output, although limited, includes Yad Vashem Studies, Torah commentaries, and nonfiction works on the history of Jewish mysticism, for example. Classic texts like *Pirke Avot* and tractates of the Talmud are also available.

Liturgical Press (Catholic)—Collegeville, MN. Based at St. John's Abbey, Liturgical Press publishes popular and scholarly works in liturgy, scripture, theology, and spirituality. Liturgical Press's scholarly line includes a well-known commentary series, Sacra Pagina, as well as resources for liturgical practices.

Orbis Books (Catholic)—Ossining, NY. Orbis Books, founded by the Maryknoll order of Catholic priests and brothers, is nearly synonymous with publications on liberation theology, peace and justice, and spirituality. Orbis is known for works about and by Thomas Merton. The press has been active in engaging Vatican II and has served as one of the early voices speaking out against injustice around the world, on behalf of the poor and disenfranchised and on behalf of migrants. It is also known for embracing a global view of the Christian faith. While Orbis Books publishes chiefly for the non-specialist, its publications are informed by current scholarship, nuanced presentations, and challenging interpretations.

Pilgrim Press (United Church of Christ)—Cleveland, OH. Touted as North America's oldest publishing operation, Pilgrim Press is a denominational press with a sweeping and inclusive author pool and audience. According to its website, "The Pilgrim Press publishes books that nurture spiritual growth, cultivate religious leadership, and provoke our collective soul for the sake of a just world." Scholars may write for Pilgrim, but most of its list is driven by tackling contemporary issues in the larger world of the church: ecumenism, gender, racism, intolerance, violence, prayer, and spirituality.

St. Vladimir's Seminary Press (Orthodox Church)—Yonkers, NY. St. Vladimir's Seminary Press publishes widely (children's books, pastoral resources, education, homily collections, and liturgy aids). It produces books and one scholarly journal in and around Orthodox Christianity. This includes books on early Christian leaders (like Athanasius, Gregory the Great, Tertullian, Basil, the Desert Fathers and Mothers) and biblical commentaries. Written for an audience beyond scholars, the volumes are nonetheless authored by scholars.

Society for Promoting Christian Knowledge (SPCK) (Anglican Church)—London, UK. The publisher of authors like N.T. (Tom) Wright (St. Andrews), Rodney Stark (University of Washington), and Rowan Williams (former archbishop of Canterbury), SPCK has had a longstanding reputation for publishing scholarly as well as more popularly targeted books. With authors from a variety of traditions and locations, SPCK commands an international audience.

Westminster John Knox; Presbyterian Publishing Corporation (WJK)—Louisville, KY. One of several highly regarded scholarly interdenominational presses, WJK has for years been at the forefront of publishing for lay audiences, professional audiences (ministers), and scholarly audiences. For scholarly audiences, WJK is heralded for its Old and New Testament Library series, its Library of Christian Classics, and its Interpretation biblical commentary series. WJK also translated the highly influential works of twentieth-century scholars like Oscar Cullmann for an American audience hungry for German scholarship. Scholars authoring volumes in these series come from a wide range of denominational traditions. Moreover, WJK does not shy away from culturally controversial topics including politics, economics, interfaith dialogue, practical theology, and race relations.

Interdenominational publishing houses and your career

If you plan to work in a religiously affiliated liberal arts college, seminary, or graduate school of religion, choosing an interdenominational publishing house could be a wise choice. Publishers like Augsburg Fortress (Lutheran), Westminster John Knox (Presbyterian USA), Abingdon (United Methodist), Orbis or Liturgical (Catholic), Jewish Theological Seminary Press, and Chalice (Disciples of Christ) carry weight. Though denominationally backed, these presses are known to be ecumenical and committed to scholarly integrity (i.e., peer review), and they tend not to publish theologically apologetic or polemical writings. Many interdenominational presses publish works that offer religious and theological perspectives on matters of social justice (e.g., immigration, advocacy for the poor), social change (e.g., accepting the LBGTQ communities into the church), racial diversity and equity, and environmental responsibility. On topics related to biblical studies, authors employ critical methods when writing commentaries, exegetical works, and theological interpretation. While these presses might have been publishing revised dissertations fifteen years ago, most can no longer afford to do it. With interdenominational publishers adapting to so many markets (church, ministers, Bible-study, youth ministries, missions, counseling, and pastoral care), "hard-core" scholarship is taking a back seat. Like most publishers, they're looking for a wider audience and more sales. We even see changes in the academic lists of these presses as they're financially squeezed out to make room for more economically viable projects. Their gaze is increasingly turned toward books that meet the needs of ministers, laity, and congregations and that address contemporary issues (practical theology).

Non-denominational publishers

If you have ever attended the annual meeting of the American Academy of Religion or Society of Biblical Literature, a walk through the exhibit hall offers a taste of the variety and the number of publishers in scholarly—and sometimes non-scholarly—religious and theological publishing. The landscape geographically, theologically, religiously, and intellectually is deep and wide, and in addition to denominational publishers, one will see non-denominational publishers. That is, some presses have a deep commitment to academic religious and theological publishing but they are not formally affiliated with a denomination or particular religious group. Familiar publishers in this category include Baker, especially Baker Academic, Eerdmans, Polebridge, Wipf & Stock, and IVP Academic. In the UK, presses like SCM (Student Christian Movement) and the Society for Promoting Christian Knowledge (SPCK), Sheffield Phoenix Press, and Paternoster (now located in Australia and owned by Koorong) are part of this group.

Let's take a quick look at the non-denominational presses on the map at the back of this *Guide*:

Baker Academic, part of the Baker Publishing Group—Grand Rapids, MI. Baker's roots in the Reformed and evangelical traditions are reflected in classic reprints like the works of Calvin, and volumes on systematic theology (e.g., Christology, Pneumatology, and the Doctrine of God). Baker Academic publishes in the areas of biblical studies, church history, practical theology, theology, and spirituality, and it targets especially Christian audiences, whether scholars, students, or professionals. Baker Academic's list includes the study of more traditional liberal arts disciplines (e.g., literature, philosophy, psychology) from a Christian perspective.

Wm. B. Eerdmans—Grand Rapids, MI. Eerdmans also traces its roots to the Dutch Reformed Church. It began at a time when co-publishing partnerships with publishers in England and Germany were commonplace. Over the years, the press expanded its list and grew in a variety of directions: biblical studies, church history, practical theology, ethics, church and ministry, classic reprints, co-publications, and reference works. Eerdmans's lists also include subjects related to the humanities and the social sciences, such as art, the environment, literature, higher education, music, poetry, business, anthropology, and psychology.

Gorgias Press—Piscataway, NJ. Gorgias is an independent academic press. It could easily be categorized as "commercial" (it partners with De Gruyter), as could others in this category, but it is relatively small, owned by an individual rather than a corporation, and relatively new (est. 2001). It specializes in Syriac-related titles and the ancient Near East as well as Eastern Christianity, and it also publishes journals.

IVP Academic—Menlo Park, CA. A subsidiary of InterVarsity Press, IVP Academic publishes under the auspices of InterVarsity Christian Fellowship, an interdenominational evangelical campus ministry. Its publications appeal chiefly to interdenominational, conservative audiences.

Jewish Publication Society (JPS; partner with University of Nebraska) —Philadelphia, PA. JPS is not a learned society but a nonprofit, nondenominational publisher of Jewish works in English. For more than 125 years, JPS has published translations of *Tanakh* [Hebrew Bible], JPS Bible commentaries, and works on American Judaism, on Midrash and Rabbinic Literature, and on everything from ancient history to women's studies to Holocaust studies to classic literature to volumes on culture, art, and music.

Lockwood Press—Atlanta, GA. Founded in 2010, Lockwood Press has established itself in the arena of ancient Near Eastern languages, literature, history, and culture. The press specializes in monographs, technical works, reference material, history, languages, and archaeology. Much like Eisenbrauns (now owned by Penn State University Press), Lockwood's success has been built upon a reputation for scholarly integrity and for understanding the fields in which it publishes particularly well.

SCM Press—London, UK. Originally associated with the Student Christian Movement, SCM Press has been owned since 1997 by Hymns Ancient and Modern. In its heyday, SCM Press was renowned for publishing theologians like Karl Barth and Dietrich Bonhoeffer as well as controversial figures like the Anglican Bishop J. A. T. Robinson, who questioned traditional Christian dogma in the 1960s of the last century. SCM introduced the English-speaking world to the works of German scholars like Martin Hengel. Scripture and early church researchers like W. H. C. Friend and James D. G. Dunn also published with SCM. After being acquired by Hymns Ancient and Modern, SCM has retreated from the forefront of scholarship, but it still maintains an active list on issues of major concern such as violence, globalization, and theological education, and on study guides.

Smyth & Helwys Publishing Inc.—Macon, GA. Smyth & Helwys publishes a wide variety of resources, from Bible commentaries to volumes on spirituality, church history, and fiction. Several volumes of Clarence Jordan's *Cottonpatch Gospel* are now publications of Smyth & Helwys. Today, among the AAR and SBL crowd, it is perhaps best known for its biblical commentary series. The series is self-described on its website as a "new commentary series . . . designed to make quality Bible study more accessible." Though Smyth & Helwys promote a Baptist perspective, it publishes authors from a variety of theological perspectives.

Wipf & Stock—Eugene, OR. Wipf & Stock is the brainchild of John Wipf and Jon Stock, both former West Coast booksellers specializing in religious and theological publications, broadly speaking evangelical. They joined forces in 1995 to form a publishing house and rapidly became a powerful presence in the landscape of religious and theological publishing. Wipf & Stock initially took advantage of print-on-demand (short run) printing to build a backlist of titles that other publishers were putting out of print. Researchers whose rights had been reverted found it easy to partner with Wipf & Stock to keep their books in print. It now has seven imprints, two of them most relevant to scholarly work: Pickwick (which published revised dissertations, monographs, and Festschriften) and Cascade Books. Hiring experienced editors, Wipf & Stock quickly built a reputation among religious and theologically affiliated schools.

> **66** Non-denominational publishers historically have played a valuable role in helping professors working in ATS seminaries and colleges.

Non-denominational publishing houses and your career

Many of these presses are recognized notably in the areas of biblical and theological studies. Many are known for commentary series, Bible dictionaries, and language resources. Non-denominational publishers historically have played a valuable role in helping professors working in ATS seminaries and colleges. Non-denominational presses often have internal and external readers who are qualified and committed to solid scholarship. Thus, at many denominational or non-denominational, evangelical institutions, these presses figure prominently in tenure and promotion.

Commercial publishers

We're using the term *commercial* to identify traditional publishers that do not historically have active ties to a particular religious or theological tradition. Commercial publishers' audiences are typically non-specialists; they number in the tens of thousands, and they read widely across a broad range of topics and issues. We're purposefully excluding those commercial publishers, like Prentice Hall or Houghton Mifflin Harcourt, that produce textbooks, as textbooks rarely count for tenure or promotion. The category of commercial publishers includes organizations that vary by size, by location and reach, and by history, as well as by the quality of their lists and commitment to scholarship. Commercial publishers distinguish themselves in that they traditionally have concentrated on selling reference works and works produced over a long duration to the library market. Even in the nineteenth century, reference works like *The Early Church Fathers* were the domain of commercial entities. T&T Clark of Edinburgh, Scotland (Presbyterian), was the original publisher of this 38-volume set. Later commercial publishers stood behind massive reference works, like Brill's *Encyclopedia of Islam*, or Brepols's *Corpus Christianorum*, or Mohr Siebeck's massive *Religion im Geschichte und Gegenwart*. Macmillan (New York) and Keter Books (Jerusalem; later acquired by Modan Publishing, one of Israel's leading publishers) joined forces to produce the *Encyclopedia Judaica*. When print ruled, commercial publishers would publish massive reference resources that libraries collected, often by a standing order title, which a library received automatically. A standing order assured the publisher of an ongoing stream of customers who annually purchased a new volume. (Presses like Oxford University Press and Cambridge University Press also employed this model in creating the reference resources like G. W. H. Lampe's *Patristic Lexicon*, H. G. Liddell-R. Scott's *Greek-English Lexicon*, later revised by H. S. Jones, and *Cambridge Ancient History*). Publishers (and not just commercial ones) adapted business models for publishing monograph series based on this model, works like Wissenschaftliche Untersuchungen zum Neuen Testament, the *International Critical Commentary*, and the *Theological Dictionary of the New Testament* (*Theologische Wörterbuch zum Neuen Testament*, Kohlhammer Verlag). And at the time, libraries' budgets were flush and they had shelves to fill. Publishers in this category also built their reputations with prominent boards, cutting-edge work, and essential books and journals. Commercial publishers were instrumental in both creating and dominating fields of study. With the discoveries of the Dead Sea Scrolls and Nag Hammadi, for example, it was commercial publishers who first invested in creating resources and made those resources profitable. But as more investors saw scholarly publishing as a way to make money, new players entered the field, some buying out businesses like T&T Clark or Continuum. This is a significant group, and it changes as publishing consolidates and contracts. (See the taxonomy at the back of this book.)

Bloomsbury Publishing—London, UK; New York, NY; and other satellite locations. Bloomsbury is a large publisher with international reach and several imprints. Bloomsbury Academic specializes in social sciences and humanities. Under the aegis of Bloomsbury Academic are imprints like T&T Clark, formerly a Scottish publishing house renowned for its church history, religion, and theology list. Bloomsbury acquired T&T Clark (along with Sheffield Academic and Trinity Press International) in 2003; Continuum, originally part of Crossroads-Continuum, a Catholic-supported press connected with Herder & Herder with offices in Germany and New York, was also acquired in 2003). Bloomsbury publishes highly regarded works like the International Critical Commentary, language resources in both Greek and Hebrew, and works on the ancient Near East. Bloomsbury's reputation helps establish it as a reliable source of scholarship from the likes of Leo G. Purdue and Warren Carter (*Israel and Empire*) or Nils Peter Lemche (*Ancient Israel: A New History of Israel*).

Brepols—Turnhout, Belgium. Brepols was established in the eighteenth century. The subjects it covers span a wide range: Medieval, early modern, and Renaissance studies, archaeology, early Christian texts (*Corpus Christianorum*), Judaism, book history and manuscript studies, the history of science, and the ancient Near East. Many of its publications are now digitized and available in a wide variety of languages (French, English, German, Flemish).

Brill Publishers—Leiden, The Netherlands. Brill has offices in Boston, Paderborn, Singapore, and Beijing, and traces its heritage to 1683. With several imprints, it publishes in a wide range of humanities, social sciences, and sciences, on subjects including international law and human rights and classical studies. In the area of religious theological studies, Brill is best known for its reference works on Islam, Judaism, Asian religions, the ancient Near East, and Christianity, as well as for monograph series in each of these areas. Brill publishes scholarly journals as well as books and reference resources. Chiefly these are purchased by research libraries. Brill has been instrumental in publishing resources that fostered, among other subjects, the study of the Dead Sea Scrolls as well as the Nag Hammadi Library. Its *Encyclopedia of Islam* has few peers.

De Gruyter—Berlin, Germany, and Boston, MA. De Gruyter, like Brill, is an established publisher in the sciences, social sciences, and humanities. It is well known for books, journals, and reference works on philosophy, classical studies, folklore studies, language and linguistics, and religious and theological publishing (especially in Jewish and Christian traditions and Islam). It also publishes some in practical theology, including the *International Journal of Practical Theology*. De Gruyter publishes in English and German.

Mohr Siebeck—Tübingen, Germany. Family-owned and highly respected Mohr Siebeck has been publishing books and journals since the early nineteenth century. In theological and religious studies, it has produced classics in the fields of ancient history, Roman law, Jewish studies, Islam, theological studies, biblical studies, and ancient philosophy. Mohr Siebeck publishes in German, English, Italian, and French.

Palgrave Macmillan (part of Springer Nature)—London, UK, New York, NY, and Shanghai, CN. Established in 2000 as a result of a merger, Palgrave Macmillan publishes academic titles in a wide range of fields. Its publishing program also encompasses numerous imprints like St. Martin's, Faber & Faber, and Henry Holt. Religious studies and theology spans the spectrum of topics from Jewish studies, Buddhism, Catholic Christianity, and Islam to Evangelicalism and atheism. Titles easily cross over into the trade marketplace.

Peeters Publishers—Leuven, Belgium. A family-owned business, Peeters offers books, journals, and databases on the ancient Near East, theology, patristics, archaeology, Judaism, Islam, and Christianity. According to its website, quality is assured in that "all publications are supervised by an editorial board and are fully and independently peer-reviewed."

Routledge—Abingdon, UK. Part of the Taylor & Francis Group, one of the largest five publishers in the world, Routledge publishes a variety of academic resources for students, instructors, and scholars of religion and theology, including textbooks, handbooks, and supplementary texts on a wide range of subjects, "from ancient traditions to contemporary religious experience and to religious themes in popular culture." Routledge has more than one hundred series in religious studies, so it covers almost every imaginable topic for studying the religions of the world: Buddhism, Christianity, Hinduism, South Asian traditions, Islam, Judaism, etc. as well as resources for investigating hip-hop and religion, violence, gender, and indigenous religions.

Rowman & Littlefield—Lanham, MD and London, UK. Rowman & Littlefield publishes edited volumes, monographs, and textbooks in a wide range of subjects in religion and theology from a variety of traditions. Recently, Fortress Academic (formerly Fortress Press) monographs are being published in cooperation with R&L. And a few university presses (Bucknell and Farleigh Dickenson) have joined R&L. The title list of R&L does not appear to associate series with particular editors or editorial boards.

Vandenhoeck & Ruprecht—Göttingen, Germany. V&R was founded in 1735. It publishes in a variety of subjects (art, architecture, communication, psychology, etc.) and is well known for its religious and theological list. It publishes in English and German, and topics include the ancient Near East, Second Temple Judaism, biblical studies, history (Christianity, Judaism, Islam, Reformation, Protestantism, German Pietism), and practical theology in a German context.

Wiley—Hoboken, NJ, Oxford, UK, and other locations globally. A formidable international publisher in a variety of formats and publication types for almost every scientific field as well as for the humanities and social sciences, Wiley enjoys an excellent reputation for its "Blackwell Companion" series of reference works ranging from topics like Assyria to Josephus to Kierkegaard and Hegel and to Derrida and Patristics. Wiley publishes numerous introductions to a variety of religions, volumes on biblical studies, historical theology, Qur'anic studies, and Buddhism, as well as books covering ethics, pastoral care, Reformation history, and comparative religion. Many of its titles are used as texts.

Commercial publishing houses and your career

Without question, many of the historic presses like Brill, Brepols, Peeters, and De Gruyter can be immensely valuable for promotion and tenure. These presses have editorial boards with international stature and prestige and maintain a strong commitment to the integrity of peer review and academic standards.

❝ Institutional/Society publishers are typically regarded as essential and reliable outlets for scholarly publications, and peer review is held in high regard.

Institutional/Society publishers

The category of Institutional/Society publishers incorporates learned societies that encompass major disciplines in and around religious and theological studies. (See the taxonomy at the back of this book.) Typically, these have a strong commitment to the peer-review process; some are members of the Association of University Presses as well as the prestigious American Council of Learned Societies. They often have book and journal programs, and it is not unusual for the society or association to partner with another press to coordinate publishing programs. Because learned societies are committed to peer review, they are usually regarded as a solid place to publish, although their abilities to reach a broader audience or the classroom can vary.

American Academy of Religion (AAR)—Atlanta, GA. This large learned society collaborates with Oxford University Press to publish the *Journal of the American Academy of Religion* and five book series. Engaging with topics like religion and culture, teaching religion, and the history of religion (of all varieties) gives this association a unique and authoritative position in the study of religion in a contemporary world.

American Philosophical Association (APA)—Newark, DE. Philosophy and religion have always found common, if sometimes contested, ground. Those working in the field of philosophy of religion or studying the likes of Kierkegaard or Kant will want to be aware of APA. APA publishes the quarterly *Journal of the APA* in partnership with Cambridge University Press.

American Schools of Oriental Research (ASOR)—Alexandria, VA. This distinguished learned society publishes books and journals concerning the study of the ancient Near East. Journal publications, now handled by the University of Chicago Press, include the *Journal of Cuneiform Studies*, the *Bulletin of the American Schools of Oriental Research*, and *Near Eastern Archaeology*. ASOR publishes the following book series: the ASOR Annual, an Archaeological Report Series, and the Journal of Cuneiform Studies Supplement Series.

American Society of Church History (ASCH)—Minneapolis, MN. A relatively small society, ASCH partners with Cambridge University Press in publishing *Church History: Studies in Christianity and Culture*, a highly respected journal that centers on the history of Christianity and its place in culture over time.

American Theological Library Association (ATLA)—Chicago, IL. ATLA is best known as a content aggregator (ATLAS), but it also has a small publishing program. In addition to conference proceedings, ATLA publishes the *Theological Librarianship* journal and a catalog bulletin. ATLA began an Open Access monograph series in 2014 for religious studies and theology scholars and librarians.

Association for Jewish Studies (AJS)—New York, NY. As the name implies, this scholarly society is devoted to Jewish studies. Its members publish widely on topics ranging from the Bible and Rabbinics to linguistics to Holocaust studies to contemporary Israel and Second Temple Judaism. The signature journal of the Association, the biannual *AJS Review*, is published by Cambridge University Press. AJS does not have a monograph series.

Catholic Biblical Association (CBA)—Washington, DC. This learned society publishes both monographs and the *Catholic Biblical Quarterly (CBQ)* journal, and while its name suggests a Catholic motivation, members come from a variety of religious traditions. *CBQ* is a highly respected quarterly journal; the CBA monograph series, according to the website, now in 55 volumes, reflects the Association's commitment to "encourage work on technical, detailed subjects, even of a restricted scope." CBA also publishes the indispensable *Old Testament Abstracts* and *New Testament Abstracts*.

International Institute for Islamic Thought—Herndon, VA. IIIT has been around since 1981. It publishes in both English and Arabic and is devoted to "carrying out evidence-based research in advancing education in Muslim Societies and the dissemination of this research through publication and translation, teaching, policy recommendations, and strategic engagements," according to its website. It publishes the quarterly *American Journal of Islamic Social Sciences*, as well as *Islamiyyat al Ma'rifah*, which is in Arabic.

Middle East Studies Association (MESA) of North America—Tucson, AZ. According to its website, "the Middle East Studies Association (MESA) is a private, nonprofit learned society that brings together scholars, educators, and those interested in the study of the region from all over the world. MESA is primarily concerned with the area encompassing Iran, Turkey, Afghanistan, Israel, Pakistan, and the countries of the Arab World from the seventh century to modern times." Cambridge University Press publishes both the *International Journal of Middle East Studies* and the *Review of Middle East Studies*. MESA does not publish a monograph series.

North American Patristics Society (NAPS)—Henderson, TN. Johns Hopkins University Press publishes the esteemed journal of NAPS, *The Journal of Early Christian Studies*. Its book series, Christianity in Late Antiquity, is published by the University of California Press.

Society of Biblical Literature (SBL)—Atlanta, GA. Arguably the premier society publisher in the broad areas encompassing biblical studies, with a history dating to 1880, SBL publishes the flagship *Journal of Biblical Literature* and the *SBL Handbook of Style*, 2nd ed., as well as a wide range of monographs and reference works in biblical studies writ large. Areas covered include biblical studies, Qumran/Dead Sea Scrolls, biblical archaeology, early Christianity, early Judaism, the Greco-Roman world, the classical world, language resources, and beyond. SBL's *Review of Biblical Literature* (RBL) is an online review of a variety of publications within the scope of SBL's mission.

Institutional/Society publishers and your career

Society publishers are typically regarded as essential and reliable outlets for scholarly publications, and peer review is held in high regard. Some societies elect to outsource their publishing (e.g., AAR) whereas others may insist on maintaining oversight of scholarly output. The scholar must exercise wisdom in choosing how a particular publishing platform could impact—positively or negatively—her or his career both in the present and in the future.

Trade religion publishers

Many presses speak of "trade publishing," and many scholarly publishers may actually have a few titles that sell more than several hundred copies. Presses refer to such successes as "trade titles." But what we mean by "trade" really defines those large publishing conglomerates whose business model for publishing revolves around printing in enormous quantities, selling to brick-and-mortar and online retailers and to popular audiences at huge discounts, and investing tens if not hundreds of thousands of dollars in sales, marketing, and advertising. Think of *Harry Potter*, *To Kill a Mockingbird*, or authors like Janet Daley or Oprah Winfrey. Most trade books enjoy wide translation into many languages. When it comes to religious and theological publishing, trade publishers, including presses like Oxford University Press, Random House, Shambhala, and Thomas Nelson often publish myriad versions of sacred texts, from the Bible, the Qur'an, the Bhagavad Gita, the Upanishads, the *Tibetan Book of the Dead*, or *Tao Te Ching*. Trade publishers tap into popular fascination with the mysterious, the unfamiliar. Consider Elaine Pagels's 1989 Vintage Publishers volume, *The Gnostic Gospels*. Not only is Pagels's book still in print (nearly 30 years), but it likely continues to sell in the thousands each year. Millions of copies have been printed. A few years ago, Reza Aslan, a professor of creative writing, broke onto the popular stage with *Zealot: The Life and Times of Jesus of Nazareth*. Controversy over this volume rattled the scholarly community as well as the talking heads on television. As is often the case, when scholars "go public" they risk criticism from fellow academics because they have failed to communicate the nuance of interpretation and presentation that is a life's work for so many. Trade publishing, even in the case of Pagels and Aslan, even in the face of tens of thousands of copies sold, probably had little to do with their securing tenure. Thus, while publishing a trade title might be an aspiration, it's probably better to do it later, when one's career and stature allows for such. Finally, almost all trade publishers work through a literary agent.

Below and at the back of the *Guide* we look at a few trade publishers:

HarperCollins—New York, NY. HarperCollins has been one of the foremost publishers in religion and theological studies since it emerged as Harper & Brothers then Harper & Row and HarperCollins. News Corp owns HarperCollins and its subsidiaries. Its website bills HarperCollins as the "second-largest consumer book publisher in the world." This global powerhouse has dozens of divisions around the world and covers almost any imaginable subject area in and around religious studies. Famous authors include J. R. R. Tolkien, C. S. Lewis, John F. Kennedy, Agatha Christie, and countless others. Bestsellers include Ian Barbour's *Religion in an Age of Science* or *The HarperCollins Study Bible* (published in cooperation with the Society of Biblical Literature). Scholars like Duke University Emerita Professor Elizabeth A. Clark or the late Marcus J. Borg (Oregon State) have published with HarperCollins, as did Henri J. M. Nouwen.

Penguin Random House—nearly 30 locations worldwide. Penguin, recognized by its famous Penguin monogram, has been around for years. It was acquired by Random House, which in turn is owned by Bertlesmann, a German conglomerate. Aside from Knopf Doubleday, its imprints include Schocken, Anchor, Pantheon, and Everyman's Library. Their authors are high profile: think of John Grisham, Jack Miles, P. D. James, or Anne Rice. When it comes to religion, authors like Karen Armstrong or Rabbi Jonathan Sacks come to mind. While these are scholarly authors, their works of nonfiction are written for a wider audience and are not necessarily contributions to new knowledge.

These once independent presses have played a huge role in religious and theological scholarly publishing: think of Doubleday's *Anchor Bible Dictionary* or its Anchor Bible Commentary series (now published by Yale University Press). Penguin Random House covers the spectrum of topics from explorations of traditional global religions to indigenous and diaspora studies.

Shambhala Publications—Boulder, CO. West Coast-based Shambhala (and its imprint Snow Lion) may be the most recognized publisher specializing in Buddhism. Texts also cover mysticism or meditation in other religious traditions, including Christianity, Judaism, Islam (Sufism), and Hinduism. It produces a few academic resources including lexical aids for Tibetan, a volume on Buddhist philosophy, and Sam van Schaik's *Tibetan Zen*, which is an excellent example of scholarly work on an important topic.

Simon & Schuster—New York, NY. S&S is owned by CBS. Trade titles in religious studies range widely, from scholarly informed volumes like UNC Professor Bart Ehrman's *The Triumph of Christianity* or Columbia Professor Robert Thurman's *Why the Dalai Lama Matters* to M. G. Anthony's *Coloring Book of Jewish Symbols* or former Professor Jerry B. and Julie M. Brown's *The Psychedelic Gospels*.

Thomas Nelson—Nashville, TN and Grand Rapids, MI. Renowned for publishing Bibles, Thomas Nelson was acquired by HarperCollins in 2012 as its Christian publishing arm and focuses on Christian content. Well-known authors include Max Lucado and Billy Graham. It publishes the *New King James Version of the Bible* in a variety of forms as well as editions of the 1611 *King James Version*. Scholarly output is quite limited.

Tyndale House—Carol Stream, IL. Controlling a significant share of the Christian market, Tyndale chiefly publishes Bibles and resources for Christian living. With lists on apologetics, prophecy, doctrine, resources for preaching, and doctrinal theology, Tyndale would not be considered a scholarly publisher. The popular "Tyndale Bible Commentary" is not a publication of Tyndale but of InterVarsity Press.

Zondervan—Grand Rapids, MI. Zondervan is a founding member of the Evangelical Christian Publishers Association and was purchased by Harper & Row in 1988. It is best known for its *New International Version of the Bible* as well as the *New Revised Standard Version*. Zondervan maintains a commitment to evangelical publishing and is effective at reaching the person in the pew.

Trade publishers and your career

Since trade publishing often reflects a summary or distillation of academic findings rather than the production of new knowledge, the value for promotion and tenure might be surprisingly low. True, publicity can be an important consideration for some groups, but ultimately scholarship, especially that of early and mid-career scholars, is expected to be original and ground-breaking. Nonetheless, as publishers of all kinds seek fewer monographs and more "accessible" manuscripts, the value of trade publishing will no doubt be rather fluid, especially in relation to one's local context.

University presses

University presses are defined as the 140 member presses of the Association of University Presses (AUP), an international organization of university presses, society publishers (like MLA, AHA, SBL; see the subsection Institutional/Society Publishers), and institutes (e.g., Brookings, RAND, IMF). Marked by its breadth of members, the AUP includes large university presses like Oxford and Cambridge as well as smaller presses like Ohio University Press. University presses, by virtue of their nonprofit mission, publish scholarly research in the arts, humanities, social sciences, and—to a lesser extent—the hard sciences. This group not only reaches a scholarly market (monographs and peer-reviewed journals) but also is characterized by more popularly written content (e.g., regionally targeted publications and books for a wider audience). A key feature that all share, especially in their scholarly publications, is a commitment to peer review. While no single standard defines peer review, the AUP's booklet *Best Practices in Peer Review* is a step in the right direction.[11]

For practical reasons, we will look at representative university presses; it may also be helpful to group presses according to an historic or existing religious affiliation because the institutions of several university presses have a divinity school, although these range widely in their religious agendas.

11   AUP's Guide to Best Practices for Peer Review can be found here: https://is.gd/Bg2dd0. See also section on peer review on p. 10.

Oxford and Cambridge University Presses—Oxford and Cambridge, UK (both have offices in New York and around the world). Historic presses with early connections to religious and theological studies include large presses like Oxford (Anglican roots) and Cambridge (interdenominational and nonsectarian). These presses publish in a wide variety of areas, but, for example, Oxford has published Bibles and resources for Bible study throughout its history, including the *New Oxford Annotated Bible* and the *New Revised Standard Version with the Apocrypha* as well as the *King James Bible*. But it also publishes critical editions of the Qur'an, including parallel texts in Arabic and English, as well as scholarly works on Judaism, Hinduism, Buddhism, new religions, and indigenous religions around the world. OUP's *Oxford Bibliographies* and *Oxford Research Encyclopedia in Religion* supplement this commitment to the scholarly study of religion and theology from almost any perspective. Cambridge likewise publishes the *King James Version* of the Bible, *The Book of Common Prayer*, and other resources for the pew. Scholarly publications on the Hebrew Bible, the Qur'an, or the Christian scriptures abound, as do works on ethics, philosophy, history, and "Buddhism and Eastern religions."

Large University Presses. In the US, several presses emerged as analogues to Cambridge and Oxford. Three presses, whose institutions also support a divinity school, followed the same model of publishing broadly in the area of religious and theological studies—Harvard, Yale, and Chicago. A quote from the University of Chicago Divinity School's website encapsulates the mission of all of these institutions and is mirrored in the publications of each of their presses: "The Divinity School and University represent an unparalleled depth of expertise in all five major world religions (Islam, Judaism, Buddhism, Christianity, and Hinduism), throughout their historical periods, and other religious movements, past and present."

The United Methodist Church has a number of institutions with divinity schools or schools of theology. Duke, a historic Methodist institution, has a significant publishing program ranging from books and journals on African studies to gender and sexuality to mathematics and science and technology. Topics in religious studies cover the world's major religions and especially religion as it intersects with culture (gay and queer studies, diaspora religions, religion, and politics). Works on traditionally sacred writings do not figure prominently in Duke's list.

Baylor University Press—Waco, TX. Under the aegis of the Baptist General Convention of Texas, Baylor University hosts George W. Truett Theological Seminary, which trains individuals for ministry, typically in the Baptist tradition. Baylor University Press, a member of the Association of University Presses, is unique among university presses in that it specializes almost exclusively in religious and theological publications. In contrast to Duke University Press, Baylor's list zeroes in on explicating and understanding sacred texts and history. Many of these publications are written by seminary professors from around the world specializing in biblical studies, theology, archaeology of the Near East, biblical languages, global Christianity, and church history. The majority of its books reflect a Christian worldview, although Baylor also publishes a handful of works on Judaism and Islam.

Catholic University Presses. Four Catholic institutions and their presses exemplify their institutions' commitments to scholarly inquiry into religion around the world but with a special emphasis on Catholicism: Notre Dame, Catholic University of America (CUA), Fordham, and Georgetown. The publications programs of each of these presses emphasize religious dialogue, public engagement, and ethics (Jewish, Christian, non-Western). Scholarly treatments of sacred texts from a variety of traditions characterize these presses, but there is also a commitment to publishing important documents and to tackling contemporary and past issues (sexual diversity, cultural context, African Americans, etc.) in the Catholic Church.

Most university presses' lists include publications in and around religious studies. Titles in this category may reflect a press's regional or national connection (e.g., religion in Ireland, religion in the nineteenth-century West). Usually the inquiries examine religion in the context of society, history, politics, and internationality, and across a spectrum of the world's major religions. The handful of presses below (remember there are 140 university presses in the AUP) have a niche in certain areas dealing with religion.

American University in Cairo (AUC) Press—Cairo, Egypt. AUC Press is "the Middle East's leading English-language academic book publisher," producing up to 50 new books each year. The largest translator of Arabic literature in the world, AUC publishes in relevant areas including Egyptology, ancient Near Eastern history, culture, and archaeology as well as the history of Egypt. AUC's series of volumes on Christian monasticism in Egypt, on Coptic saints, on Coptic civilization, and on the Coptic church has few peers. Investigations of Islamic and Middle East studies round out AUC's offerings in and around religion.

Amsterdam University Press—Amsterdam, The Netherlands. A small but important privately owned press, Amsterdam has a religious studies list that reflects the history of Dutch expansion into the rest of the world. Thus, one will find titles in Dutch and English on religions in Malaysia, Indonesia, and Southeast Asia. Leiden University, a short train ride from Amsterdam, is recognized as an early center for the study of Islam. That connection between Holland and its former colonies persists with several ongoing series on Islam, not only in Holland but also in other places like Turkey, Lebanon, and China. Amsterdam also examines contemporary religion in Dutch society (e.g., the emergence and impact of Pentecostalism in The Netherlands).

Columbia University Press—New York, NY. Columbia's religion list spans everything from religion and food to religion in India, Muslim approaches to politics, religion in American politics, religion and the environment, and religion and Chinese society. Books explicitly on or about the Bible seem part of Columbia's earlier history, but recently those are fewer. History of early Christianity or early Judaism has tapered off. Islam and Middle East religion are becoming strong areas of interest. Several reference works on Islam, Judaism, and Asian studies are noteworthy.

Hong Kong University Press—Pokfulam, Hong Kong. Publishing in both Chinese and English, Hong Kong University Press is recognized for Asian studies and cultural studies. As one would expect, China becomes the point of intersection for many volumes. Titles such as *Christian Women in Chinese Society*, *Christian Encounters with Chinese Cultures*, and *The Virgin Mary and Catholic Identities in Chinese History* underscore this approach. Of course, Asian religions (Confucianism, Daoism, Buddhism) as well as philosophy, history, and culture also figure prominently in any discussion of religion in China.

Indiana University (IU) Press—Bloomington, IN. IU Press enjoys an impressive reputation in Jewish studies. Areas include cultural studies, Holocaust studies, religion and cinema, anti-Semitism, Arab-Jewish relations, Ladino literature, poetry, and lexicons for Yiddish, as well as works on the Hebrew Bible, the Talmud, Midrash, biblical narrative, and rabbinic literature. Indiana also publishes widely on Islam, but the emphasis falls on social, political, and cultural matters, although these can never be fully divorced from religion.

Johns Hopkins University (JHU) Press—Baltimore, MD. Johns Hopkins bills itself as the oldest university press. Religion is covered, but typically these titles mirror other strengths of JHU Press's list in science and medicine. Its coverage crosses centuries, reaching back into the ancient world and forward to today's, but JHU seems to have resisted getting in deep when it comes to the major religions. It remains well known, however, for volumes from the Center for Anabaptist Studies.

McGill-Queens University Press—Montreal, QC. McGill-Queens situates religion in society and has a strong tradition of examining religion and pluralism, ethics, politics, and gender across Eastern and Western religious traditions. A handful of titles are of national interest (e.g., *For Canada's Sake: Public Religion, Centennial Celebrations, and the Re-making of Canada in the 1960s*).

New York University (NYU) Press—New York, NY. NYU Press publishes cutting-edge works on religions and society, African-American religion, non-Western religions, literature and religion (Jewish, Christian, Islam), and histories of religion and their impact. NYU Press has one of the finest Arabic Literature lists around. Race, politics, cinema, religion in America, and gender studies feature prominently. Jewish studies includes topics like the Holocaust, the history, culture, and stories of Jews in New York, and a few comparative works.

Penn State University Press—University Park, PA. With the acquisition of Eisenbrauns Publishers in 2017, Penn State University Press dramatically expanded its publications in religion, the ancient Near East, and archaeology. Eisenbrauns' list included biblical studies, Near East archaeology, history, and culture, and linguistic resources in and around Judeo-Christian tradition. Series on Quakers and Anabaptists and African Religions as well as early Christianity are further expanding their reach. Journals as well as book series on religious studies also figure prominently in Penn State's list (e.g., *Journal of Africana Religions*, *Bulletin of Biblical Research*, and *Journal of Eastern Mediterranean Archaeology and Heritage Studies*).

Stanford University Press—Stanford, CA. Stanford publishes on religion from a variety of perspectives including Jewish studies, religion and philosophy, history, religion and politics, and religion and society. The scope of Stanford's lists seems to acknowledge the inseparability of religion from what's happening in the larger world, whether in Latin America, in the Middle East, or right next door.

University of California (UC) Press—Berkeley, CA. UC Press covers the major religious groups plus comparative religion, indigenous religions, Taoism, and religion and popular culture. The Press's scope runs the gamut from the ancient to contemporary, from national to global. The breadth of its books and journals on a broad list of religious topics is remarkable. Its titles sometimes slip into the "trade" category (e.g., Peter Brown, *Augustine of Hippo*, or Andrew Greeley, *The Catholic Imagination*). UC Press's Luminos series reflects its strong commitment to Open Access publishing.

University of Hawai'i Press—Honolulu, HI. As one might imagine, University of Hawai'i Press produces works related to religion in Japan, China, Korea, and South and Southeast Asia, including topics on Buddhism, Protestant Christianity, Islam, indigenous religions, Catholic Christianity, Daoism, Shintoism, and Japanese philosophy, among other topics.

University of North Carolina (UNC) Press—Chapel Hill, NC. UNC Press publishes widely in religious studies, including works on Christianity, Judaism, Islam, religion in Latin America, indigenous religion, and religion in the ancient Greco-Roman world and Africa. Not surprisingly, race and religion receive special attention (e.g., *Religion and the Racist Right: Origins of the Christian Identity Movement*), as does religion and the culture of the South (e.g., *Beyond the Crossroads: The Devil and the Blues Tradition*).

University of Toronto Press (UTP)—Toronto, ON. UTP touts itself as "Canada's leading academic publisher." Its religious studies list emphasizes Canadian religion traditions, especially in Jewish studies and on topics (philosophical, political, cultural) related to the Christian church, both Catholic and Protestant. Its list includes a few impressive works related to the Bible (e.g., Northrop Frye, *The Great Code: The Bible and Literature*), but it produces only a few works directly related to the great sacred texts of the world's religions themselves, except for the *Collected Works of Erasmus* (in more than 60 volumes). In ancient Near Eastern studies, UTP can boast *The Royal Inscriptions of Mesopotamia*. UTP also lists quite a number of the publications of the eminent Canadian Jesuit priest Bernard Lonergan.

University presses and your career

Publishing with a university press should ensure a quality, peer-reviewed publication. Obviously, certain presses may carry more prestige and thus impact for tenure and promotion. Scholars should weigh many factors: (1) what kind of publication counts for promotion and tenure, (2) which press matters for promotion and tenure, (3) with which press does my project fit, and (4) which market does this press serve? The *Guide* and the map included at the back of this book should be a good starting point.

❝ Subsidy is no longer a dirty word when it comes to publishing peer-reviewed scholarship.

Miscellaneous

This informal category covers several types of publishers, a few potentially viable and a few others potentially hazardous. Some publishers turn a manuscript into a book but they may not always attend to the other aspects of publishing such as selling, marketing, sending out for review, attending conferences, etc. Some might even be called "predatory." Predatory publishers, well-known in the journal world, also exist in the book world. A *Slate* article by Joseph Stromberg sets out extremely well the scope and nature of this kind of publishing.[12] In the book space, their strategy is not so much charging you to publish your book but counting on authors to (1) give away their rights and (2) buy back copies of their own work. These publishers generally do little if anything in the way of copyediting, proofreading, marketing, selling, or promoting your work. To help scholars navigate the crowded publisher space as Open Access gains traction and credibility, there are resources like the *Directory of Open Access Journals* that help scholars identify legitimate publishing open access opportunities.[13]

Excursus: The reality of subsidy

With the shrinking of library budgets and a shift away from collecting print, the financial foundations of scholarly publishing were rocked. Publishers saw a relatively predictable market shrink if not disappear. Anecdotally, publishers spoke of the good old days when they would

---

12   Joseph Stromberg, *Slate*, Future Tense, "I Sold My Undergraduate Thesis to a Print Content Farm: A trip through the shadowy, surreal world of an academic book mill." 23 March 2014.

13   The Directory of Open Access Journals (DOAJ) and the Directory of Open Access Books (DOAB) include a list of legitimate open access publishers, here https://doaj.org/ and here: https://www.doabooks.org/.

sell 1,000 copies of a book—typically a monograph—to libraries. Today, that number is closer to 250 copies. As a result, many legitimate and highly respected publishers require subventions or subsidies to offset the high costs of publishing monographs.[14] Presently, it is not unusual for a publisher to ask a scholar for institutional support, especially if the book is lengthy or complicated or contains color. Subsidy is no longer a dirty word when it comes to publishing peer-reviewed scholarship.

The emergence of Open Access, likewise, inverts the model for how publishing works, shifting the costs from the user of content to the creator of content in the dominant model. Practically speaking, that means that the author pays to publish in an Open Access environment. For books, funding may come from agencies like Andrew Mellon or may be raised from libraries (Knowledge Unlatched). As long as the projects are peer reviewed, whether for a book or journal, it shouldn't matter that something is published Open Access. The trend is for more Open Access publishing, not less. One should, however, be wary of some of the offers to publish your work that seem to come out of nowhere or that seem too good to be true.

Self-publishing

The phenomenon and allure of self-publishing, rendered possible by new publication and distribution technologies and infrastructure, have altered how books are published and how authors think about reaching an audience. Self-published authors do have success stories, notably in genres like literary fiction and romance, but these are not academic books. For academic publishing, self-publishing lacks one critical ingredient—peer review—and therefore should be entered cautiously as part of a career publication strategy.

---

14 A 2016 study by Nancy Maron, et al., "The Cost of Publishing Monographs: Toward a Transparent Methodology" (New York: Ithaka S+R, 2016) suggests that the group average cost for a typical monograph among university presses is $30,000–$49,000, with the highest cost monograph averaging approximately $66,000–$129,000 across different-sized presses.

CHAPTER FIVE

finding a home for your project

Identifying a publisher

Given the large number of publishers working in the space of religious studies and theology, and the amorphous and expansive nature of the field, identifying the right publisher can not only save you time but also help you find the *right* home for your project and meet your professional objectives. Having indexed the main types of publishers in the preceding chapter's taxonomy, we would now like to spend some time discussing strategies for evaluating them. What criteria should scholars use when assessing whether a publisher might be a good fit for their projects and career aspirations? How should they go about researching publishers? How should they approach a publisher?

By way of preface, identifying the right publisher takes work up front but can potentially save you time and effort later, and it is critical for the success of your work. Just as one would research a potential employer when applying for jobs, scholars need to do robust research on the publishers to understand a publisher's presence, audience, and market, and to develop a strategy for pitching their projects.

Creating a long list of potential publishers

We recommend starting by creating a list of potential publishers that fit your topical interest and career goals. The taxonomy of publishers in religious and theological studies that we developed and that appears on the inside back cover of this *Guide* is a good starting point for helping you identify publishers. Look also at your bibliography and on your shelves—the publishers of the works that you are citing in your work are likely to be potential publishers for your manuscript. Tap the collective knowledge of your network and your colleagues to learn about where they are publishing and what they know about the presses in your field. Don't hesitate also to speak to editors at conferences to learn about their areas of interest, new series that they may be launching, etc. Such conversations can be very insightful and can supplant publicly available information, giving you a fuller view of a publisher's interests.

Researching and evaluating potential publishers

Once you have your long list, the next step is to research the presses more deeply and to evaluate whether there is a fit with your project. The key things to understand are each publisher's list, audience, and market. The knowledge that you gather at this stage will also help you craft your pitch to the publisher.

What should you look for when evaluating publishers? The ideal publisher for your project should have—or be actively trying to establish—a presence and interest in your subfield and on your topic. From a practical point of view, presence in the field indicates that your publisher is plugged into the community for which you are writing; it already has access to the right marketing and distribution channels and to the right audience. Scholars are understandably tempted to go with the most prestigious publisher, but in some ways it is more important to publish with the *right* publisher for your project—one who would increase the reach of your scholarship.

To establish the areas of focus of a publisher, look carefully at its list—that is, the subject areas in which it publishes. Editors spend a tremendous amount of time and effort building their lists and calibrating them as scholarship evolves, so the list is a good resource to help you get a clear picture of a publisher's topical interests. That said, it is not a complete picture: because books and series often take years to launch, the current list might not reflect, for instance, editorial plans that are underway to build presence in a new topical area or to pull out of another. Speaking to editors and colleagues could help fill in those blanks.

When looking at a publisher's titles, scholars should evaluate not only the topics on which it publishes but also the methodologies and approaches employed in its books. Look especially carefully at new and recent titles: as explained above, the list can change over time as presses continuously finetune their editorial strategies, which means that a groundbreaking book published a decade ago may no longer reflect the publisher's focus. For that reason, it is also useful to look at a publisher's blog or press releases (e.g., for new series) as well as the conferences the publisher has attended and plans to attend, as that might give you an indication of its editorial plans.

Consider also the publisher's audience and market. This question, along with a fit for the list, are the first two questions an editor would ask herself when reviewing a submission. To give you a real-life example, albeit one from commercial non-fiction: Rebecca Skloot, the best-selling author of *The Immortal Life of Henrietta Lacks*, famously posted on Twitter a collage of the rejection letters she received from publishers. While her post was about perseverance, it is noteworthy that almost all of the rejection letters expressed lack of certainty about the fit with the list and the alignment with the audience/market. When evaluating publishers, consider whether a publisher caters to the audience your work is targeting. For instance, if you've written a scholarly monograph, you would want to focus on publishers who have a foot in the academic market, and avoid trade publishers.

> **"**At the end of your research, you should have a clear idea of the list, audience, and market of the publishers on your long list, and enough overall information to begin narrowing it down and prioritizing your choices.

Establishing fit

The first question that editors ask themselves when reviewing a submission is whether it fits the list and how well it aligns with its audience/market. **It falls on you to make the case that your work would strengthen the list as much as it would benefit from it.** With that in mind, it is worth spending some time to familiarize yourself with the publisher's list and to situate your work within it. Consider how your work fits within the intellectual conversation that the list weaves together. Does it complement it? Does it fill a gap? Does it build on conversations already started by the titles on that list? Does it explore new approaches to the problem? It falls on you to persuade the publisher that your work is a good fit and publishing choice, and this information will help you develop a strong argument.

At the end of your research, you should have a clear idea of the list, the audience, and the market of the publishers on your long list, and enough overall information to begin narrowing it down and prioritizing your choices.

Multiple submissions

It is worth knowing that submission to multiple publishers is allowed for book projects (never for journal articles). Etiquette, however, requires you to disclose upfront whether your work is under review at other presses. Further, if an editor agrees to send your manuscript out for review, because reviews are a financial and time investment for publishers, the expectation is that you would inform all the other presses to whom you've sent your manuscript.

Approaching a publisher

The next step in the process after you have identified the right publisher(s) is approaching and pitching your idea. In this section, we'll discuss the process and the etiquette of approaching a publisher. This part of the process can be confusing and intimidating; in the context of an oversaturated market, where supply of research and manuscripts exceeds demand by publishers, understanding the process and publishers' expectations can empower scholars and equip them with knowledge to be more productive.

When to approach a publisher

When to approach a publisher is one of the most commonly asked questions that publishers receive. Many publishers require a proposal (discussed below) and one or two sample chapters for submission; they typically would expect to see the full manuscript before offering a contract, especially from early-career scholars without a long publications track-record. Other publishers, with an interest in broader topics for larger audiences, may wish to start the conversation before the manuscript is complete.

That said, you may start the conversation at different stages—when you only have an idea, when you have a partially written manuscript, or after your manuscript has been completed—but your approach may be different in each of these scenarios. In all three, however, by the time you approach a publisher you will have identified publishers of interest, whose lists your project would both fit with and strengthen.

- **Approaching at the idea stage.** It is never too early to start a conversation with an editor, so it is acceptable for you to start "shopping" your project and soliciting interest when it is at the idea stage. The benefit of starting the conversation early is that you can receive preliminary feedback about areas of interest for the press, or advice on how to shape your project in a way that would appeal to the publisher. There is no guarantee that the publisher will be interested

"In the context of an oversaturated market, understanding the process and publishers' expectations can empower scholars and equip them with knowledge to be more productive.

in pursuing your project; that will depend on your manuscript as well as on the publisher's areas of focus at the time of submission, which could be years later. This approach comes with two caveats: (1) Even at this early stage, you should have a fairly fleshed out—if not final— idea of what you're offering and why it would be a good fit for the given publisher. (2) You should have a plan and follow up on it.

- **Approaching with a partially completed manuscript.** You may also approach when you have a partially written manuscript. The benefit of this approach is that at this stage you are likely to have a fleshed out idea, a robust argument and well-formulated statement about its importance, and a nuanced and critical understanding of the literature, as well as the ability to speak to the unique selling points of your project. You're therefore well-equipped to make a compelling argument as to why your project would be a good fit. If approaching with a partially written manuscript, it is helpful to have a concrete and realistic plan and timetable for its completion.

- **Approaching when you have a complete manuscript.** In many cases, and particularly so with early-career scholars who have not yet built a robust publishing record, the publisher will typically want to see the full manuscript before making a decision. (With senior scholars with a robust publication track record, there may be more flexibility.) A reminder: when submitting, read carefully the submission guidelines and follow them closely. Frequently, those are tied to internal processes, workflows, and staff that ensure that your manuscript is processed quickly. More subtly, following the rules signals your professionalism to editors.

Preparing your submission materials

This part can be confusing and intimidating especially if it's a new exercise for scholars and authors. Below we'll look at the details of preparing a proposal.

The proposal normally consists of the following components:

1) A brief synopsis or description of the project

- **Topic.** Describe succinctly the topic of your work and the rationale for it. What is your thesis? When explaining how it fits within the intellectual conversation, do not forget to explain what its implications are and why it is important. A word of caution: one of the more common rationales we see in proposals is "it has not been done before." This rationale in and of itself isn't sufficient reason to justify publication and entry in the scholarly record. Focus instead on the implications and importance of your work (e.g., this project is important because, . . . it challenges/updates/broadens/etc. our understanding of ...). If your work fits within a larger cultural conversation or could be tied to an event like an anniversary, do your best to strengthen that connection. Sometimes the success of a project depends on its timing and the cultural wave it rides.

  It is also necessary to delineate the parameters of your project—its aims and scope, so to speak. What is included in it, and why? What is out of scope, and why? Are there any chronological limits to your project? Any methodological restrictions? Explain your choice.

- **Approach.** Discuss the approach, methodology, or theoretical framework of your work. What is the purpose of your book, and how will it help you achieve that purpose? If appropriate, discuss how your approach is distinct from related works on this topic.

- **Unique features.** Take the time to touch on the distinctive and unique features of your work. Those selling points should help distinguish your work from existing titles.

Is your work interdisciplinary in new and innovative ways? Does it rely on unique, important, and heretofore unstudied archives? Is it global in orientation and framed in that way? Is its approach or methodology innovative? Do you have a unique perspective?

2) Apparatus

Describe whether the book will include information about images, artwork, or special features like sidebars, case studies, datasets, glossaries, references, etc.

3) Status of the work

Provide information about the status of the work. Be specific and realistic: if it's partially written, how many chapters exactly are completed? How many more remain to be completed, and what specifically remains to be done? How long will it realistically take you to complete it? A word of caution: It's tempting to be overly optimistic about how long it will take when you are pitching your project and want to grab the editor's attention, but in this case it's more important to be realistic. Publishers plan their budgets and allocate resources based on estimated project dates, and they might line up, say, reviewers or a production team based on your estimate. What matters to them more than an ambitious submission schedule is a realistic publication schedule and the author's ability to stick to it.

4) Competing/related titles

You should use this section to explain how your book fits within the intellectual conversation and current scholarship. Provide a thorough yet concise assessment of related titles that are on the market, their strengths and weaknesses, and how your work differs and expands on existing works. This is also a good place to highlight the contribution your project would make and to explain how it would advance knowledge.

5) Market and audience considerations

Being vague or unclear about audience and market is a common reason for rejection. Who are the potential readers? In what disciplines are they situated? What is the potential of course adoption? Be realistic in your description of the target audience and market: a monograph can rarely both serve its primary specialized audience *and* be an ideal textbook. Questions that scholars ask are not always the questions being asked by communities of faith.

6) Annotated outline

Regardless of the completion status of your book, you should prepare an annotated tentative table of contents or outline that summarizes in detail the focus and content of the proposed chapters and their scope, and their estimated or actual length. While different publishers' requirements might vary, typically the chapter descriptions should be about a paragraph long. Pay particular attention to articulating the book's organization (e.g., is it divided in parts or sections, are the chapters subdivided into subsections, what are the proposed headings, etc.), as it helps the editor to see how the individual chapters fit together as a book.

7) Abstract

The abstract is a concise version of the project description, intended to give readers a basic idea of the work. Well-written abstracts that skillfully weave in a synthesis of the argument with unique features and that underline the importance of the research—why does it matter?—hook the readers in more than descriptive summaries.

8) Sample chapters

9) Author CV

10) Cover letter

Your prospectus should be accompanied by a cover letter. The purpose of the cover letter is to seduce the editor to continue reading and to position yourself as an engaged and professional author. As a marketing document, the appearance of the cover matters tremendously in an industry as formal as publishing, so do take care to include the necessary formalities and to proofread it. The contents of a successful cover letter should consist of (1) a concise project description, with attention given to its unique features; (2) a clear statement about the importance of your research—the "so what?" question; (3) a focused and persuasive explanation of how your work fits with and would strengthen the press' list; (4) a nuanced understanding of the audience and market of the publisher and how it relates to your project; and (5) a short bio establishing your credentials and suggesting why you are well-positioned to write this book.

What editors look for

The appearance of your submission is the first impression that an editor will get of you and your work. In that regard, appearances and form matter. Be sure to submit a clean, well-written, and professionally compiled manuscript that reflects the submission instructions carefully.

As we've underscored above, the first main consideration for editors is the extent to which a submission is a good fit for the list and for the audience and market of the publisher. It falls on you to offer a convincing, well-articulated, and thoroughly researched statement about both of these. Further, the editor evaluates the contents of the submission. Manuscripts written for broader audiences or on topics of broader appeal, in accessible prose, are preferred to jargon-laden, narrowly specialized books. The editor also considers the amount of revisions that might potentially be necessary. While editors don't shy away from revisions, in some cases (e.g., if the writing lacks clarity, or the organization of the work is too confusing, or if it is written for an audience different from

> **"** Publishers are looking for engaged, knowledgeable, and professional authors and are not solely interested in content.

the stated one), rejection might be the logical and pragmatic decision. If, conversely, the editor sees potential, she may send it out for review and make a decision based on the feedback.

In all of these cases, however, publishers are looking for engaged, knowledgeable, and professional authors and are not solely interested in content. We hope that this *Guide* equips you with sufficient knowledge to navigate the scholarly publishing world in your career.

conclusion

We constructed and wrote *The ATS Guide to Religious and Theological Publishing* with essentially a single, yet highly diverse, audience in mind: administrators and faculty members of the nearly 280 institutions that constitute The Association of Theological Schools. This is a wide-ranging group of institutions and individuals, and we've sought not to oversimplify the complexity of the different faith commitments and circumstances for faculty at these institutions. Taxonomies, however, often require oversimplification. Faith orientations span from Southern Baptists to Pentecostals to United Methodists and Reformed to Anabaptists, Catholics, and Unitarians. The *Guide* examines and categorizes the scholarly publishing religious and theological landscape most relevant to these groups. As far as the publishers on the map located on the inside back cover of the *Guide*, we've given the most attention to those centered on the Judeo-Christian tradition, but we have not ignored the religious and theological traditions outside of that tradition. The *Guide* is not exhaustive. The target audience, like ATS itself, is mainly North America; moreover, the publishers represent only a fraction of the publishers who publish in these areas. Nevertheless, the principles underlying the taxonomy and presented in the *Guide* as a framework for establishing a publishing strategy and selecting a publisher can be applied to publishers not covered here. The *Guide* offers guidelines and provides some shortcuts, but the work of creating a strategy, writing a manuscript, identifying a publisher, and approaching a publisher falls to you, the scholar. Not covered in the *Guide*, but equally vital to the scholarly career, are topics such as the place of clear and cogent non-academic writing. These cannot be overstated. A full understanding of how peer review works in a given field, likewise, should be a tool in one's toolbox.

❝ The *Guide* offers guidelines and provides some shortcuts, but the work of creating a strategy, writing a manuscript, identifying a publisher, and approaching a publisher falls to you, the scholar.

It should also be remembered that the *Guide* is "fixed," but the world it describes is not. That is, publishers will continue to be bought and sold, and in that exchange, publishers will change. Denominations will change their own emphases and may increase or decrease their commitments to scholarly inquiry. What once was a great press may become a mediocre press; what once was questionable may rise to new standards of scholarly excellence and reputation. Furthermore, the requirements for tenure and promotion have heretofore only risen, as the number of academic positions decreases. The days of a revised dissertation counting as one's first book are nearly gone. New experiments in the role of digital production as it relates to tenure and promotion are already underway. Nonetheless, it seems clear that the expectations around publishing for obtaining an academic position will only increase, just as it is clear that a robust publishing track record affords more choice of professional opportunities. Thus, it is imperative that early and mid-career scholars construct a viable publishing strategy. Scholars must also resist inadvertently painting themselves into an ideological corner by making poor publication decisions, in terms of either what they publish or where they publish. The *Guide* is designed to assist scholars in building their strategies for a successful career.

bibliography

A select bibliography related to scholarly publishing, writing, and the academic career.

Career-related Teaching, Promotion, Tenure, Publishing

Alexander, Patrick H. "The Less Obvious Elements of an Effective Book Proposal." *Chronicle of Higher Education* 17 October 2011. http://chronicle.com/article/The-Less-Obvious-Elements-of/129361/.

_____. "What Just Ain't So." *Inside Higher Education*. 6 April 2009. http://www.insidehighered.com/views/2009/04/06/alexander.

_____. "Your Dissertation is Done. Move On." *Chronicle of Higher Education*. 1 September 2014. https://is.gd/H45AMB.

American Academy of Religion. https://www.aarweb.org/employment-services/additional-resources.

American Anthropological Association, Career Center. http://www.aaanet.org/profdev/index.cfm.

American Historical Association. http://www.historians.org/.

American Philosophical Association, Career Resources. http://www.apaonline.org/?page=career.

Blum, Hester. "Show 'em Who You Are." *Inside Higher Education.* 11 September 2013. http://www.insidehighered.com/advice/2013/09/11/essay-seeking-job-academe.

Cassuto, Leonard. "The Rise of the Mini-Monograph: Is it senior professors, rather than administrators, who are most reluctant to embrace midlength e-books for tenure? *Chronicle of Higher Education* 12 August 2013. http://chronicle.com/article/The-Rise-of-the-Mini-Monograph/141007/?cid=at&utm_source=at&utm_medium=en.

Crowder, Stephanie Buckhanon. "Too Few To Lose." *Huffington Post.* 27 June 2017. http://bit.ly/2siKm9U.t

Fitzpatrick, Kathleen. *Planned Obsolescence: Publishing Technology and the Future of the Academy.* New York: NYU Press, 2011. http://www.plannedobsolescence.net/kathleen-fitzpatrick/.

Housewright, Ross, Roger C Schonfeld, Kate Wulfson. "Ithaka S+R US Faculty Survey 2012." http://www.sr.ithaka.org/research-publications/us-faculty-survey-2012.

Harley, Diane, Sophia Krzys Acord, Shannon Lawrence, and Elise Herrala. "Peer Review in Academic Promotion and Publishing: Its Meaning, Locus, and Future." Center for the Study of Higher Education. March 2011. http://cshe.berkeley.edu/publications/publications.php?id=357.

Kelsky, Karen. "The Professor is In: Tenure Expectations." *The Chronicle of Higher Education.* Vitae. 23 February 2015. http://bit.ly/1EMm4B8.

————. *The Professor Is In: The Essential Guide to Turning Your Ph.D. into a Job.* New York: Three Rivers Press, 2015.

Linguistic Society of America, Jobs Center. http://www.linguisticsociety.org/jobs-center.

McCutcheon, Russell. "Theses on Professionalization." *The Religious Studies Project.* 29 February 2012. http://bit.ly/1hCXTPM.

Report of the MLA Task Force on Evaluating Scholarship for Tenure and Promotion. 2007. http://www.mla.org/tenure_promotion.

Satell, Greg. "Why Communication is Today's Most Important Skill." *Forbes* 6 February 2015. http://onforb.es/18ZvSO8.

Saussy, Haun. "Reviewing Scholarly Books." *Printculture: Media, Culture, Politics, Academic Life, Weasels* 25 August 2013. http://printculture.com/reviewing-scholarly-books/.

SBL Career Resources. https://www.sbl-site.org/careercenter/jobs.aspx.

Steel, Colin. "Scholarly Monograph Publishing in the 21st Century: The Future More Than Ever Should Be an Open Book." *Journal of Electronic Publishing* 11 (2, 2008): http://dx.doi.org/10.3998/3336451.0011.201.

Toor, Rachel. "The Reality of Writing a Good Book Proposal." *The Chronicle of Higher Education* 11 February 2013. http://chronicle.com/article/The-Reality-of-Writing-a-Good/137207.

————. "How to Write a Good Book Proposal, the Sequel." *The Chronicle of Higher Education* 8 October 2013. http://chronicle.com/article/How-to-Write-a-Good-Book/142183/.

Weiss, Bob. "Five Tips for Successful Joining." http://apps.americanbar.org/lpm/lpt/articles/mkt1103.html.

Publishing/Scholarly Communication

Brown, Laura, Rebecca Griffiths, and Matthew Rascoff. 2007. "University Publishing in a Digital Age" (so-called Ithaka Report).

Thompson, John. *Books in a Digital Age: The Transformation of Academic and Higher Education Publishing in Britain and the United States.* London: Polity, 2005.

Copyright and Intellectual Property

Aufderheide, Patricia, Peter Jaszi, et al. "Copyright, Permissions, and Fair Use among Visual Artists and the Academic and Museum Visual Arts Communities: An Issues Report." The College Art Association, 29 January 2014 (http://bit.ly/1p9UaXO).

————, and Peter Jaszi. *Reclaiming Fair Use: How to Put Balance Back in Copyright.* Chicago: University of Chicago, 2011.

Bielstein, Susan, M. *Permissions: A Survival Guide: Blunt Talk about Art as Intellectual Property.* Chicago: University of Chicago, 2006.

American Library Association: http://www.ala.org/advocacy/copyright/pattersonaward/patersonbib.

American Theological Library Association: https://atla.libguides.com/copyright/home.

Code of Best Practices in Fair Use for the Visual Arts. February 2015. http://www.collegeart.org/fair-use/.

Consortium of College and University Media Centers (CCUMC). "Fair Use Guidelines for Educational Multimedia": http://www.adec.edu/admin/papers/fair10-17.html.

Concerning Governmental Copyright Reform: http://www.uspto.gov/news/publications/copyrightgreenpaper.pdf.

Copyright Clearance Center: http://www.copyright.com/.

Cornell's Copyright term chart: http://copyright.cornell.edu/resources/public-domain.cfm.

Creative Commons Licensing: http://creativecommons.org/ ; esp. http://creativecommons.org/licenses/.

Crews, Kenneth D. *Copyright Law and Graduate Research: New Media, New Rights, and Your Dissertation.* Ann Arbor, MI: UMI, original edition 1992; revised 1996 and 2000.

"Hearing on the Scope of Fair Use: House Judiciary Committee. Subcommittee on Courts, Intellectual Property and the Internet." http://judiciary.house.gov/index.cfm/2014/1/the-scope-of-fair-use.

"Public Access to Public Science Act." Introduce in the House 20 Sept. 2013. See http://beta.congress.gov/bill/113th-congress/house-bill/3157.

University of Texas. "Crash Copyright Course." http://copyright.lib.utexas.edu.

Library of Congress. http://copyright.gov/.

Stanford's site on fair use and copyright: http://fairuse.stanford.edu/.

Writing/Style

Adler, Mortimer J., and Charles Van Doren. *How to Read a Book.* Revised and updated. New York: Touchstone, 1972.

Alexander, Patrick H. [Pressed, I. M. D.] "Scholarly Writing under Siege." *CSSR Bulletin* 28 (4, 1999): 126–31.

Baker, Sheridan Warner. *The Practical Stylist with Readings and Handbook.* 8th ed. New York: Longman, 1998.

Bennett, Drake, "Thinking Literally: the surprising ways that metaphors shape your world." *The Boston Globe.* September 27, 2009. http://www.boston.com/bostonglobe/ideas/articles/2009/09/27/thinking_literally/.

Berlin, Isaiah. "The Divorce between the Sciences and the Humanities." Pages 80–110 in *Against the Current: Essays in the History of Ideas.* Edited and with a bibliography by H. Hardy. London: The Hogarth Press, 1979.

Boice, Robert. *Professors as Writers: A Self-Help Guide to Productive Writing.* Stillwater, Okla.: New Forums Press, 1990.

_____. *How Writers Journey to Comfort and Fluency: A Psychological Approach.* Praeger, 1994.

Bolker, Joan. *Writing Your Dissertation in Fifteen Minutes a Day: A Guide To Starting, Revising, and Finishing Your Doctoral Thesis.* New York: Henry Holt, 1998.

Brooks, David. "Meeting the Editors." *The Chronicle of Higher Education.* 9 May 2011.

Brown, Scott. "A Guide to Writing Academic Essays in Religious Studies." *CSSR Bulletin* 28 (3, 1999): 69–76.

Burchfield, R. W., ed., and Henry W. Fowler. *The New Fowler's Modern English Usage.* 3d ed. Oxford: Clarendon Press 1996.

Burnam, Tom. *The Dictionary of Misinformation.* New York: Crowell, 1975.

The Chicago Manual of Style: The Essential Guide for Writers, Editors, and Publishers. 16th ed. Chicago: University of Chicago Press, 2010. Available online: http://www.chicagomanualofstyle.org/home.html.

Cassuto, Leonard, "From Dissertation to Book." *The Chronicle of Higher Education.* 30 May 2011.

_____. "It's a Dissertation, Not a Book." *The Chronicle of Higher Education.* 24 July 2011.

Cook, Claire Kehrwald. *Line by Line: How to Improve Your Own Writing.* Boston: Houghton Mifflin, 1985.

Corral, Will H. "Beware the Language Police." *The Chronicle of Higher Education.* 11 July 2003. http://www.chronicle.com/weekly/v49/i44/44b00501.htm.

Derricourt, Robin. *An Author's Guide to Scholarly Publishing.* Princeton: Princeton University Press, 1996.

Dillard, Annie. *The Writing Life.* New York: Harper, 1990.

Fowler, Henry W. *Dictionary of Modern English Usage.* 2d ed. Oxford: Oxford University Press, 1965.

Fulford, Robert. "They Should Know Better: Humanities Scholars Spend Lots of Time Reading, So Why Can't They Write?" *National Post.* Tuesday, 15 July 2003. http://www.robertfulford.com/2003-07-15-humanities.html.

Germano, William. *Getting It Published: A Guide for Scholars and Anyone Else Serious about Serious Books.* Chicago: University of Chicago Press, 2001.

————. *Dissertation to Book: How To Turn Your Doctoral Thesis into Something More.* Chicago: University of Chicago Press, 2003." The Chronicle of Higher Education April 22, 2005. http://chronicle.com/weekly/v51/i33/33b02001.htm.

Gordon, Karen Elizabeth. *The Deluxe Transitive Vampire: The Ultimate Handbook of Grammar for the Innocent, the Eager, and the Doomed.* New York: Pantheon, 1993.

Greenbaum, Sidney. *The Oxford English Grammar.* Oxford: Oxford University Press, 1996.

Groff, Kent Ira. *Writing Tides: Finding Grace and Growth through Writing.* Nashville, Abingdon Press, 2007.

Hayot, Eric. *The Elements of Academic Style: Writing for the Humanities.* New York: Columbia, 2014.

Holdrege, Barbara A. "The Emperor's New Clothes: Writing the Dissertation as a Book." No date or pages. Online: http://www.jv-site.org/topic/miscellaneous/hold.html.

Hornstein, Gail A. "Prune That Prose: Learning to Write for Readers beyond Academe." *The Chronicle of Higher Education.* 7 September 2009. http://chronicle.com/article/Prune-That-Prose/48273/.

Jackson, John L. Jr. "Turning Dissertations into Books." *The Chronicle of Higher Education.* December 14, 2009. http://chronicle.com/blogPost/Turning-Dissertations-Into/9208/.

Jasper, James M. "Why So Many Academics Are Lousy Writers." *The Chronicle of Higher Education.* Tuesday, 26 March 2002. http://wiredcampus.chronicle.com/article/Why-So-Many-Academics-are/45990/.

King, Stephen. *On Writing.* New York: Pocket, 2002.

Lamott, Anne. *Bird by Bird: Some Instructions on Writing and Life.* New York: Anchor Doubleday, 1994. Lindberg, Christine A. The Oxford American Thesaurus of Current English . Oxford and New York: Oxford University Press, 1999.

Lepore, Jill. "The New Economy of Letters: The Chronicle Review." *The Chronicle of Higher Education.* 3 September 2013. http://chronicle.com/article/The-New-Economy-of-Letters/141291/?cid=cr.

Miller, James. "Is Bad Writing Necessary? George Orwell, Theodor Adorno, and the Politics of Literature." *Lingua Franca* 9.9 (December/January 2000). http://linguafranca.mirror.theinfo.org/9912/writing.html.

Miller, Naomi J. "Following Your Scholarly Passions." *The Chronicle of Higher Education.* 25 March 2002. http://chronicle.com/article/Following-Your-Scholarly/45988/.

Murray, Rowena. "Writing for an Academic Journal: 10 Tips." *The Guardian: Higher Education Network* 6 September 2013. http://www.theguardian.com/higher-education-network/blog/2013/sep/06/academic-journal-writing-top-tips?CMP=twt_gu. From idem, *Writing for Academic Journals.* 3d edition. Berkshire, UK: Open University Press.

O'Connor, Patricia T. *Woe Is I: The Grammarphobe's Guide to Better English in Plain English.* New York: Putnam, 1996.

Olson, Gary A. "It Is Who You Know and Who Knows You." *The Chronicle of Higher Education.* 10 January 2010. http://chronicle.com/article/It-Is-Who-You-KnowWho/63560/.

Orwell, George. "Politics and the English Language." In *A Collection of Essays.* San Diego: Harcourt Brace, 1946. Available on the internet at http://www.k-1.com/Orwell/pol.htm.

Plotnik, Arthur. *The Elements of Editing: A Modern Guide for Editors and Journalists.* New York: Macmillan, 1982.

Pressed, I. M. D. "Scholarly Writing under Siege." *CSSR Bulletin* 28 (4, 1999): 126–31.

Rowson, Richard C. "The Scholar and the Art of Publishing." Pages 226–37 in *The Academic's Handbook*. Edited by A. Leigh Deneef, Craufurd D. Goodwin, and Ellen Stern McCrate. 2d ed. Durham, N.C.: Duke University Press, 1995.

Savage, William W. Jr. "'Times Ain't Now Nothin' Like They Used to Be,'" *Journal of Scholarly Publishing* 34 (3, April 2003) 146–52.

Savage, William W. Jr. "Scribble, Scribble Toil and Trouble: Forced Productivity in the Modern University." *Journal of Scholarly Publishing* 35 (1, 2003) 40–46. http://muse.jhu.edu/journals/journal_of_scholarly_publishing/v035/35.1savage.html.

The SBL Handbook of Style: For Biblical Studies and Related Disciplines. 2d ed. Atlanta: SBL Press, 2014.

Stainton, Elsie Myers. *The Fine Art of Copyediting.* 2d ed. New York. Columbia University Press, 2002.

Strunk, William, Jr., and E. B. White. *The Elements of Style.* 3d ed. New York: Macmillan, 1979.

Sword, Helen. "Zombie Nouns." *The New York Times* July 23, 2012. http://opinionator.blogs.nytimes.com/2012/07/23/zombie-nouns/?src=me&ref=-general.

Toor, Rachel. "My Little Bag of Writing Tricks." *The Chronicle of Higher Education.* 3 September 2013. http://chronicle.com/article/My-Little-Bag-of-Writing/141309/.

_____. "Scholars Talk about Writing: Sam Wineburg." *The Chronicle of Higher Education.* 17 August 2015. http://bit.ly/1JcM2Cz.

_____. "Bad Writing and Bad Thinking." *The Chronicle of Higher Education* April 15, 2010.

_____. "Goodbye to All That." *The Chronicle of Higher Education* March 24, 2008. http://chronicle.com/jobs/news/2008/03/2008032401c/careers.html.

_____. "The Habit of Writing." *The Chronicle of Higher Education* February 11, 2010. http://chronicle.com/article/The-Habit-of-Writing/64001/?sid=pm&utm_source=pm&utm_.

_____. "Think of Yourself as a Writer." *The Chronicle of Higher Education* March 7, 2011.

_____. "A Publishing Primer." *The Chronicle of Higher Education* August 11, 2008.

Williams, Joseph M. *Style: Toward Clarity and Grace.* Chicago: University of Chicago, 1990.

_____. *Style: Ten Lessons in Clarity and Grace.* 7th ed. New York: Longman, 2002.

Zinsser, William. *On Writing Well: The Classic Guide to Writing Non-Fiction. 30th Anniversary Edition.* New York: Collins, 2001.

_____. "Writing English as a Second Language." *The American Scholar* December 1, 2009. http://www.theamericanscholar.org/writing-english-as-a-secondlanguage/.

_____. *Writing to Learn.* New York: Harper Perennial, 1993.

index